Said the Earth, Lord of the
Shining Face: my house is empty,
send thy sons to people
this wheel.

(*The Book of Dyzan* 4:17)[1]

---

[1]*Secret Doctrine*, H.P. Blavatsky. In Sanskrit, Dhyanas (Dyzan)
means meditation or contemplation.

LORD OF THE SHINING FACE: MY HOUSE IS EMPTY

by

Margaret Kirk

Published by

𝔾 ARTEMIS BOOKS 𝔾

Nevada City, California

1997

On the Cover:
"Day of the Dead" by Menlo Macfarlane, 1989
Pastel on Arches paper, 11" X 15"
Interior illustrations, book and cover design by Lily Nova
Edited by Iven Lourie and Lily Nova

Lord of The Shining Face: My House Is Empty
by Margaret Kirk

Copyright© 1997 by Margaret Kirk
All Rights Reserved. Printed in Canada by
   Hignell Book Printing Ltd., Winnipeg, Canada
   First Printing: November, 1997
Library of Congress Catalog Card Number: 97-74400

ISBN: 0-9645181-0-4

Published by

Artemis Books

Tel: (530) 271-2239
Fax: (530) 272-0184
Orders: (800) 869-0658
email: info@gatewaysbooksandtapes.com

LORD OF THE SHINING FACE: MY HOUSE IS EMPTY

CONTENTS - OVERVIEW

ACKNOWLEDGMENTS

I wish to thank all those friends who helped me believe that I could become a writer. I am indebted to my daughter, Joyce Quaytman, who had the courage to read the material raw and rough, then confidently suggest changes. Thanks go to my first editor, Deke Castleman, for showing me the way, and to J.J. (Juanita Judson) for introducing me to Grass Valley and Artemis Books, headed by Iven Lourie and Lily Nova, who have now created this book around my words.

Maggy Kirk

Author's Introduction

In *Lord of the Shining Face: My House is Empty* myth, legend, fable, and history regarding the origins of our world are woven together. My message to you, the reader, emerges as a gentle assault against the various patent approaches commonly used to explain our world and the thing we call "life." These existing explanations are both narrow and show a disdain for the elements of truth found in the oral histories of many cultures. It is simpler and, perhaps, much less painful to accept the adroitly fashioned concepts of pure evolutionary theory or creationism than to wrestle with integrating these varied and often unsupported ideas from the past into our belief systems. It is possible that the "truths" of evolutionary theory or creationism are no less fallible than those contained in the stories of the ancients, however. It is also possible that the "fact" of evolution or the Biblical account of creation, spoon-fed to us in our infancy along with strained spinach and applesauce, is merely another mask to hide the face of ignorance.

We have among us some who profess to hold the ultimate answers to these questions and they usually attract a large following of those who long for easy answers to assuage their fears about existence. I do not pretend to have any unusual knowledge, just a passion for truth, and the injured feeling that I am being kept in the dark where the complete history of the world and its beginning is concerned. In this writing, by tapping a good deal of "unscientific" lore, I am attempting to present a more complete picture of the origin of Man, genus Homo Sapiens Sapiens. I am saying: Life on Earth may not—in fact, quite possibly did not—begin in the Garden of Eden. Man's time on this planet seems to be much longer than our Biblical history would have us believe, as the evidence of the evolutionist maintains. But, again, did this highly sophisticated form of life emerge from a quiver of energy and a streak of lightning? I propose that evolution is only a part of the picture, and, in this picture, genetic engineering may have taken the role of Creator.

The gods that are part of our established religious doctrines are also found in ancient writings which depict them as highly knowledgeable or powerful men. Our gods knew the wonders of the universe and accessed scientific abilities far beyond anything the human had even dreamed. Many ancient as well as modern religions assert that Man was made in the image of a god, with the powers to create miracles. Is Man dimly aware of this? Today the UFO's which stir our imaginations seem to prove that the gods are still watching over the world that they created...they may walk among us.

In seeking the answers to our origins, I have found that these answers have a way of turning into other questions. Here are a few: Is Earth a cosmic colony constructed (created) by universal engineers? Was this universal construction designed for a new breed—Man? Or was this construction begun to serve as an outreach station for the housing of wanderers, adventurers, or universal pioneers? Whatever the reason, my question is: Are we living on a universal space station and are we the descendants of those gods? Today we are finding this possibility especially intriguing since our own engineers are now creating planet Earth's early steps into space. Maybe these god-like ancestors are watching us follow in their footsteps. "The Watchers" was the name the Egyptians gave to "those gods that came down from the sky."[1]

In the following chapters, I will first speak of my own intense curiosity about these questions, my need to know, which fueled the writing of this book. Later you will get acquainted with my research and musings about the early gods of earth, their humanness and various functions here on earth. I will then try to provide a new perspective on the construction of planet Earth, as well as explore my doubts that either evolutionary theory or creationism can fully explain our existence. In the following material, I will conduct something of a physical examination of the human, searching for that all important but elusive spiritual element. From there we will engage in an account of UFO's, their controversial presence in our skies, and the questions these "objects" provoke as to our beginnings. The final chapter looks at the "impossibilities" of today's world which may become ordinary, even mundane, in the world of tomorrow.

Finally, these words of introduction must rightly end with a saying from the prophet Isaiah: "Come, let us reason together." [2]

---

[1] According to Sitchin, *The Stairway to Heaven*, p. 111, the term Neter (Watchers) was used by the Egyptians to refer to the gods that came down from Heaven and their landing place on Earth, Sumer.

[2] A Hebrew prophet of the 8th Century B.C.; source: *Douyay Bible*.

WHO AM I...?

I am a Thing
    Earth and Heavenly Fire
A Something
    Small Dot in the Span of Eternity
A collection of Atoms
    A Speck of energy

I am Me
I am You
I am It and Them
    And Those
    All who move on belly
    foot or wing

I am a Patch of Sky
A Lump of Soil
A Grain of Sand
A Spray of Salt Sea
A Disciple of Heaven
    With the Kiss of Hell
    on Rose Petal Lips

It seems true
    I am indentured to a Master—
    One of Miracles
And Heavenly Angels watch
    while shadows beckon
    Luring me into Deep Waters

No Solon smiles on me
No Wise Man guides me
    I am lost in a labyrinth
    Caught between Two Worlds
    Yesterday and Tomorrow

My Soul sleepwalks
    across a Wasteland of Time
    Calling out

    Who am I
    Why am I here
    Where am I going

                M. K. Kirk

1
WHAT MAKES THE WORLD TICK?

*I would like to step outside the conditioning maze and see what
makes it tick. I wonder what I would find.*

*Perhaps a terrible superhuman monstrosity the very contem-
plation of which would make a man insane?*

*Perhaps a solemn gathering of wise men? Or the maddening
simplicity of unattended clockwork?*

(Taken from *Patterns of Reinforcement* by Ferster and B.F.
Skinner)

Like Ferster and Skinner I wanted to know what made
this world "tick." This book started with that need to
know; a need to find answers to questions like: are we the
end product of a lowly lump of clay and a single authoritative decision? "Let us make man in our image?" Or—
perhaps, a spontaneous life form spawned by a dazzling
burst of incomprehensible energies? To evolve from this
into a high form of thinking animal? Or are we, perhaps
descendants of cosmic forefathers—with universal connections—Earth, a new frontier for a people from another
star?

From childhood on, there was this deep curiosity. A
need to find solutions other than the old "truths" that were
automatically spooned out to all, young and old alike, inquiring minds.

Like a mathematician I expected to be able to chalk
across the blackboard of experience a logical, viable formula for the evaluation of existence. And like many, I refused to accept Webster's casual definition of life: "...a
period of existence...the quality that distinguishes a vital
and functioning being from a dead body or inanimate

matter." This does not answer those age-old questions: Who am I? Where did I come from? Where am I going? And the most bewildering—Why?

Men of science demanding a systematic approach, nimbly skip over the persistent question of "why are we here?" playing around with the "who are we?" bit; giving out statements on the quantity of water, minerals, red corpuscles, and white corpuscles. They probe the brain but never discover a mind. They take man completely apart and find nothing that can be recognized as a soul.

The games that man plays to comfort the mind, a support for a belief that there really is a known purpose to life, appears, under scrutiny, to be nothing but a highly designed, and programmed, conformity. This has been the subject of many books, old books coming out of ancient minds and beliefs, and the new, written by our learned men and women, in the recently established fields of science. But the same program is still, today, being used as an answer to the question of man's place in the universal scheme of life. Perhaps it is necessary to satisfy our physiological needs. The spiritual self has to make do with whatever it can pick up in a game-playing material world.

According to P.D. Ouspensky, "Man lives a life under two different kinds of influences." [1] The first are interests and attractions created by life itself; health, money, and pleasures; security, pride and fame. The second kind are interests of a different order that generally come out of schools. In this way the persuasion of many different minds come to man through philosophy, science, and religion.

---

[1] *The Psychology of Man's Possible Evolution*, P.D. Ouspensky.

The linear movement of past, present, and future— sunrises and sunsets—and the measurement of parts in between, accord man a possible succession of partitioned experiences. These events never quite come together as a total but seem to remain a summarized line of fractioned postulates that supposedly explain life. The past is stored in the mind, becoming a memory that is nostalgically reviewed whenever a similar experience occurs. It's just like opening that old trunk in the attic. Man's *now* is spent straddling the present—one foot in the past and the other hesitatingly moving into the future. Much of that hesitation is based on the knowledge that if he moves too far into the future there is no longer any need to deal with the other two segments of his brief career—he will be dead. This he fears. But it is part of man's culture to accept this fact without trying too hard to understand it, because this, he is also afraid to comprehend.

What would be the impact on man and his present life if he believed that his jobs—or adventures here on Earth were only part of a lifetime. How would it change his thinking? His actions?

Man has been plodding along for the last ten million years (we think) without much in the way of progress. Unless one counts the number of times man has risen to a point of success only to be thrown back spiritually, physically and scientifically into another beginning. A *where do I go from here?* point.

The reasoning is always the same: Why am I here? Where am I going? For what reason? Is there a real meaning to life? Is there a real reason for life on Earth? Have I missed something that others know? If I have who can enlighten me? Religion? Science? It seems that when man stops at this point and starts asking questions he is in trouble. He is only one of the millions of Earthly humans asking the same questions. But he is alone. He lives alone and dies alone with the questions still unanswered. Lately, in this twentieth century, man is asking another question: Am I part of a vast universal program, a dependent of a higher civilization?

In considering the possibilities of a beginning for man and his world, Earth, there are those who would have us still cling to the old theory of something out of nothing. The materialization of whole universes out of a void. Creation. Evolution. The two theories coming out of science and religion are separated only by their practitioners.

Man has been suckled on the *wine of immortality*; its euphoria or numbing effects easing the pain of that baffling period of birthing, growing and dying that we call life. But with the death of the paternalistic father figure that has been passed down from generation to generation, existential withdrawal has set in leaving us with a lack of any panacea for our anxieties.

It is becoming more evident that our world and its humans were not born out of a solitary word—a single bit of magic. Creation of a planet and its people does not fit, realistically, into this type of operation. And as we become more and more scientifically aware, we are digging up evidence that makes us realize man did not reach his high form of thinking-animal status through evolution. Now we are asking: Where do we look for our salvation?

Those who would have us believe in a God creator see the design and apparent purpose of this world as evidence of a Wise Supreme Being. This much I will agree with. This small cosmic world—plane of existence, perhaps an outreach colony—must have been designed and constructed by universal intelligence. I feel that with the advent of the now present unidentified flying objects—our so-called UFOs—there is no longer any question of other civilizations, it's other intelligent life. The presence of advanced, noiseless space craft in our skies attests to a cosmic life force.

Neither theology nor science has been able to explain to my satisfaction, man and the part he and his world play in the universal picture—his beginning nor his reason for being. This manuscript poses questions of a strong current interest for a specific audience. It is asking: Were there really gods in the beginning of our world? Did man, quite possibly, exaggerate the preeminence of those god-like beings and their miracles? And did we have story-tellers among the cave dwelling survivors who, like those of today, performed for the excitement and applause of an audience? Who magnified the event? Glorified a common experience to satisfy hungry minds?

I have never been anything but an interested outsider peering over the shoulder of recognized science. But I have always been an intelligent spectator, one who from this sideline position was able to realize that the many experts were running around with bits and pieces of the same puzzle in their possession; always loudly denouncing any other part as impossible. Today for the sake of sanity, there seems to be a need to bring together all those bits and pieces into a believable formula.

The purpose of this book is to provide a synthesis of legend, scientific data and philosophic inquiry for the consideration of any curious mind that has questioned current theories. The author believes this approach will make it possible to fill in some of the missing pieces between Von Daniken's conjectures about extraterrestrials, Auel's *Clan of the Cave Bear* and Edgar Cayce's "readings"—as he described them.

In this writing I have tried to resurrect those ancient questions through myths and legends, histories and old manuscripts coming out of the many different cultures of our world. Some are primitive and simple, such as those taken from Fahs and Sporel's *The Beginnings*. Others are specialized studies such as Gurdjieff's works, and Ouspensky's, including his *A New Model Of The Universe* and the exploration of earth and space as covered by Emmanuel Velikovsky in his *Earth In Upheaval*.

In this book I am considering these questions: Was the big bang really a BIG BANG or was it an explosion of a single star in only one part of the universe? Was the world created by a gaseous explosion or a god? Or gods?

Von Daniken's theories talk about gods (plural) as do many ancient writings including the *Popul Vuh* (the Mayan bible), the CABALA (Kabahla, Kabala), the EGYPTIAN BOOK OF THE DEAD, the Hindu VEDAS, and our own western BIBLE. I also found informative material in reference books and data coming out of today's science publications, such as the information on quantum mechanics and the government sanctioned studies of UFOs as found mainly in Captain Rapel's (head of the government operation) *Blue Book*.

The audience I expect to reach is of this world, people who have found our present day contemplations on man and his planet unsatisfactory, unfulfilling, and decidedly without any logical foundation. A tired old theme that has been played too long, too loud, and at the wrong movie. It does nothing toward calming our fears, healing our anguish.

We have many theories regarding man and his world. But it's all theory. We are all making educated (and not so educated—sometimes emotional) guesses, theorizing rationally or otherwise. Life cannot be explained scientifically. It can only be dealt with theoretically. Eventually with the broadening of our own horizons we will recognize the potential of our assumed "impossibilities." We will be able to understand the probability of many different worlds with, quite possibly, as many different life-forms. We are not alone in a many galaxy, universal cosmic world. Velikovsky (*Earth in Upheaval*) reminds us:

> Science today, as in the days of Newton, lies before us as a great uncharted ocean, and we have not yet sailed very far from the coast of ignorance.

We try to employ facts—human's mathematical reality—to measure the immeasurable. It shows us that the mind of man still operates on much the same principle as it did when man thought the Earth was flat. But today, after hundreds of years of a kind of mental stagnation, drastic changes are being made in the lifestyle of the Thinking Man. Old beliefs are being threatened. We, as a group, are beginning to have doubts about the so-called "norm" of our society. Maybe because of this we are discovering something about ourselves.

We are now getting into the realization that we are, scientifically, very young; our tools for measuring our universe are inadequate. Almost childlike. And we are learning that perchance there is only one "impossible" that is possible. We are beginning to realize that in making a statement "impossible," as the mysteries of our ever expanding universe unfold, we are, at that point, getting into

11

the area of the real impossible. In as much as an untutored, small universal species, who is right now struggling to achieve the ability to use ten per cent of its potential, claims to have the knowledge to place labels on the unusual.

Once, not too long ago and at a time when it was considered impossible, Christopher Columbus sailed across an unknown body of water. At that time it was believed that the earth was flat. Columbus and his crew, according to the authorities of that day, would drop right off the edge of the world. That is, if they weren't first devoured by very large sea monsters. To be a leader takes courage. Many followed Columbus after he had shown them that the earth was not flat and the sea monsters were in the minds of men.

The things that were yesterday considered impossible and are today in common use would be almost impossible to list, but to name a few: the automobile (that god-awful-mechanical-contraption that would never replace the horse); the telephone, the electric light and the radio. How about television? (It's ridiculous! Imagine such tomfoolery? Pulling a picture right out of the air? Indeed!)

Fulton was considered a fool because of his interest in steam as a form of power. The possibility that steam would one day replace sails on ships was roundly criticized by the authorities of the day and placed in the category of impossibilities—a "pipe dream." But nevertheless, steam was to that era what gasoline is to our modern conveyance system.

Hidden among the many patents in our government office lies the genius of Tesla, inventor and futurist. His impossible claim that electricity lay under our feet, in the earth, there for the taking, gave him the name of an eccentric. Even after proving his theory it was still said to be impossible. Yet in archeological excavations, lights have been found burning. They may have been burning for hundreds—maybe even thousands of years. Their energy source? The earth.

What about tomorrow? What impossible things will be a common part of our future? UFOs landing on Earth? UFOs bringing citizens from other worlds—other than Little Green Men?

Man has an insecurity that allows—even demands—that he ridicule that which his limited imagination cannot grasp. He prefers the confines of fenced-in cults that offer comfort by body count alone, to permitting his imagination to guide him into the darkness of the "Great Unknown."

Up to a few years ago I spent my time much like the majority of my fellow man, being chased by a minute hand and constantly in debt to the mechanical guardian of the hours. Then some Angel of Mercy gave me a wonderful book. I had read books before. I enjoyed books. They were especially nice to get involved in when I was trying to ignore the face of the monster that was busily ticking off my time. It was on a day of this kind that I opened the book.

"Dare to think!" flew out at me. I was slightly startled to say the least by this unprovoked attack. A stranger had entered my life and cast aspersions on one of my natural processes. But my eyes moved along. My mind opened up and there came from that stranger, the small churning sound, the opening of a tightly closed door, creaking on rusty hinges. The voice went on to speak to a now alert mind: "Don't be afraid to face facts, and never lose your ability to ask questions: Why? and How? Be in this like a child." Emanuel Velikovsky was getting through to me.

I was nine years old when I started asking "embarrassing" questions. To my young, logical mind, adult things did not always make sense. Adults, to my way of thinking at that early age, were not always very smart. The answers that I received from the authority figures did nothing to change my opinion, but they had the upper hand—they were bigger than me.

About that time nourishment for a hungry imagination sailed into my life with Jules Verne's "impossible" underwater craft. While the Nautilus plied its way from bookstore to bookshelf, we of the younger generation took time to observe the eager acceptance and indescribable wonder of the grown-ups as they moved eagerly into a future of practical "impossibles" brought into being by the inventions of Thomas A. Edison.

With the origin of the comic strip Buck Rogers, we, the youth of that era, had our very own *impossibility* to brighten our days. A hero came into our lives. With the aid of a mysterious pack strapped securely to his back, this man of our future world could sail up into the air— high above the rooftops of the cities and their inhabitants. The astonished faces were always directed upward— roundly circled words hanging above the gaping mouths. To a childish, creative mind, Buck's manner of travel made very good sense. It was a wonderful way to bypass all the clutter and noise of trolleys, and other generally uncomfortable modes of transportation. The idea that it should be considered impossible never entered our minds. The only question was: How did he do it? However, our enthusiasm was often dampened by the humorous, but generally loving, condescension of our elders. It was, they would declare knowingly, absolutely impossible.

Grandmama's heart could never have survived television. Let alone watching, on that impossible "instrument of the Devil," a man walking upon the moon. Grandma looked upon the electric iron as an enemy. Something that was there to "mess up" her life.

Looking back on all this makes me totally indebted to Velikovsky, a great thinker, and others like him who have the courage to step into the unknown; opening doors so that others like myself can follow, for having helped me to be something other than a hypnotized member of a dusty, if not dead, society. From that book to this one I have demanded answers; haunting bookstores and libraries; seeking out those minds eloquent on different perspectives. Thoughts, beliefs—ancient writings that had, generation after generation, been ignored by many religious cultures.

In turn, I am hoping that this book will open a few minds, perhaps stimulate the imagination of a commercially stagnated culture. I am openly asking the questions: Are we really the sculpted image of a god? Maybe a clone? Could it be possible that we emerged from a single bit of watery life and evolved into a thinking land animal who is now capable of destroying his own world? Or are we part of a Cosmic Universal System, pioneers on an Outreach Space Station—Earth, fashioned by Universal Designers whom we call gods?

Using what we know as a rational approach to a theory, and based on our modern science and recent history, we might see Earth as a universal penal colony. Such as Australia was to England. A place for those who upset the "norm" of a society. That would not be hard to believe considering what goes on in our "civilized" world. Or, if not that, maybe a weather, message, and outside guard station such as we support in the arctic? Or, to allow ourselves a bit of humor, how about considering Earth as a play pen for the young and precocious—with gods as baby-sitters? I am not trying for answers, just new perspectives.

What do I believe? I believe that Earth is a space world. Built—constructed or created—by universal engineers. A space station, part of an existing universe; a new settlement for a new species. I am inclined to think that man's confusion as to life and its meaning, was brought on by more than one destruction caused by natural forces. Every culture has stories of more than one catastrophe. Here is one that comes out of the legends of the Dacca and Haishai Indians[2]:

> The gods left the earth at hour zero, 1048 B.C., according to the calendar of the white barbarians. They gave the starting signal for the new epoch in the history of my people who faced a terrible time after the gleaming ships of the earlier lords were extinguished like stars in the heavens....

And the Dashai Indians claim this is the fourth world:

> ...Tuwagachi, World Complete...It has everything to choose from. What you choose will determine...whether it must be destroyed too...

I do believe that man's beginning on Earth was kept alive by those surviving the catastrophes. It was passed

---

[2]Legend of the Dacca and Haishai Indians (1048 BC). *Gold of the Gods*, Erich Von Daniken.

down from generation to generation by the story tellers, each time embellished and given a more magical and fabled beginning for the benefit of those lost humans who needed to believe that their progenitors had not deserted them. As time passed the stories grew and those men of science became even greater—larger than life—more awesome to the simple minds hearing the words of the storytellers.

I believe that our many stories centered around gods comes from an early contact with universal beings—a small glimpse of a cosmic world. A scenario woven around men from another galaxy. Or even another part of our own galaxy. We hear this from Euhemerus (400 B.C.), "Gods of the old religions were simply deified men about whom myths and traditions cast a halo of divinity.[3]"

After each destruction—maybe hundreds or thousands of years—according to Zechariah Sitchin (*The Stairway to Heaven*) "When the waters subsided and the Annunaki (Sumerian gods) began to land on Ararat...", the gods performed what to the eyes of survivors were miracles. Earth was brought back into livable condition: (Genesis 1:12)[4] "...and the earth brought forth grass, the herb yielding seed and the fruit tree yielding fruit...." These were the gods that were remembered. But they were not gods. They were men. They were highly advanced universal inhabitants. There are many stories coming out of the different cultures—some will be found in another chapter—about gods landing on Earth. One such is a Sumerian legend speaking of the god Anu who came down into the valley of the Euphrates and established our present civili-

---

[3] Greek writer 400 B.C.
[4] *Holy Bible,* King James Version.

zation[5]—that is one that can be found in the British Museum in London.

A world designed and constructed by gods does sound like a myth to an Earthbound human. But it really is the same story as the one that is found in the Old Testament. Perhaps this is a myth—one built upon a foundation of an actual event, removed from realism by elaboration, superstition, and time.

Perhaps today, as we move into the twenty-first century, we will be able to see the possibility of just such a new world, our new world, a space station. The plans for this are right now moving across the boards of our government engineers. A giant wheel moving in space housing ten thousand Earth humans—adventurers, space pioneers. Our shuttles were designed to be the covered wagons of the space age.

Expounding on a new hypothesis or theory may at times be unpopular but is nonetheless not unusual. All that we today consider a very practical part of our lives, may have been, in one of our yesterdays, an unpopular theory. Like evolution. Any explanation that man has been playing around with—dealing with his life here on Earth—has come out of a theory. A theory not based on facts, but generally on another theory which in turn comes out of still other speculations, principles, philosophy, or doctrines.

Most of the problems that come out of a venture of this kind are not so much the concerns with the destruction of old beliefs, but deal more with the obstacle course

---

[5] *Gods, Graves and Scholars*, C.N. Ceram. Legend on stone tablets in an excavation site near Babylon found by English archeologist Sir Charles Leonard Woolley in 1929.

set up by man's fence-building. I must find my way through a verbally constructed categorical maze. I can only touch on the many subjects that became a part of my research. Many books have been written on all these subjects. My intention is not to explain any one but to bring them together as interlacing parts of a puzzle. The difficulty lies in bringing this material from the many different sources into a readable format that, hopefully, excludes confusion.

In this book I am not trying to answer the unanswerable. I am merely putting forth a personal belief that has been reinforced by my research into ancient writings, histories, myths, and legends. I am bringing it together with the findings of our modern science and in this way producing a new perspective on the history of man and his world. I wish to present a new probable as to man's beginning and existence. To look again but from a new position, at the old questions: Where did man come from? Why is man on a planet—plane of existence—called Earth? Where is he going? And—who and where are his creators, his gods?

> ...he who gives breath and thought...who watches over the happiness of the people, the happiness of the human race...who meditates on the goodness of all that exists in the sky, on the earth, in the lakes and in the sea....[6]

---

[6] *Mayan Book of the Dawn, Popul Vuh,* the Mayan bible, translated by Dennis Tedlock.

GODS

Ancient Deities

Cosmogonical Deities
Primordial Beings
Male/Female Principle, Androgynous
Deities of the Universe, Space
Supreme Being, Great Spirit, High
God/Creator Deities

Celestial Deities
Sky and Heaven Gods
Solar Gods: Dawn, Day, Light, Twilight, Eclipses
Lunar Gods: Eclipses
Gods of Night, Darkness
Stellar Gods: Constellations, Planets, Stars

Atmospheric Deities
Weather Gods: Thunder, Lightning, Rain,
Wind, Rainbow, Drought

Terrestrial Deities
Animal/Bird Gods
Earth Gods: Land, Soil Earthquakes
Fire Gods: Elemental, Domestic
Fresh Water Gods: Rivers, Lakes, Irrigation,
Curative Waters
Metals: Mines, Minerals, Treasures
Nature Gods: Forest, Hills, Mountains,
Stones, Trees
Sea Gods: Surf, Coastline, Seafarers,
Navigation

Life/Death Cycle Deities
Life: Birth, Procreation, Soul (in life),
Longevity
Mankind: Men, Women, Children, Youth,
Age
Fertility: Animal, Vegetable, Phallic
Disease Gods: Accident, Illness
Death Gods: The Dead, Soul (in death),
Funeral, Embalming, Cemeteries
Afterworld/Underworld: Judgment,
Soul (in death)
Resurrection/Rejuvenation Deities

Economic Activities
Agriculture/Vegetation Gods
Deities of Domesticated Animals
Fishing: Fish Gods, Water Animals
Household Gods: Doors, Hearth, Home, etc.
Hunting: Gods of Wild Animals
Roads & Locations: Crossroads,
    Boundaries, Gates, Travelers
Trades & Crafts: Merchants, Markets,
    Artisans
Gods of Wealth: Abundance, Plenty,
    Prosperity
Gods of Non-Wealth: Famine, Hunger,
    Poverty

Socio-Cultural Concepts
Abstract Deities
Arts: Music, Dancing, Poetry, Theater
Gods of the Cardinal Points
Culture: Teachers/Givers, Lesser Creator
    Gods
Gods of Evil, Destructiveness
Gods of Destiny, Fate
Fortune: Luck, Good or Bad
Intellectual: Wisdom, Learning, Teaching,
    Scribes, Records, History
Justice: Law, Judgment, Equity,
    Government, Order, Morals,
    Oaths, Curses, Thieves
Love: Lust, Sexuality, Phallic, Lovers
Gods of Marriage
Medicine & Health: Body, Healing, Herbs,
    Senses
Pleasures: Happiness, Revelry, Festivals,
    Games
Gods of Time & Seasons: Calendar
Gods of War: Victory
Gods of Wine: Intoxicants, Narcotics,
    Drunkenness

Religion
Religious Activities: Rituals, Initiation,
    Ceremonials, Divination, Prophecy
Magic, Sorcery

2

GODS

(Webster) **god**, n. 1. god; 2. god O.E., M.E. *god*; common GMC., but it probably represents an Aryan neur. P.P. type ghu-tom; cp.Scrt. *huta*, that to which sacrifice is made:...l.a. any of a class of powerful spirits regarded as controlling a department of nature or of human activity, and as such generally worshipped.

...one becomes a god only by finding worshippers.—C.G. Jung[1]

There was a time in the history of man when every part of nature had its own god. The stars, the moon, and the sun played important roles in early man's picture of those gods to whom all of nature was indebted. To those humans there was meaning in the appearance of a star that shone divinely through the branches of a tree, or was seen as hanging prophetically over a rooftop or mountain pinnacle.

The lonely sound of an owl, the cry of a wolf, a peal of thunder; each was significant according to the intensity of the performance—a roar or a whisper—and the beliefs behind the interpreter. All were voices of the gods.

Wind moving through the trees, a flash of lightning, these were considered opinions, or the judgements of gods. The benevolent gods were sent thanks in prayers

---

[1] Carl Gustav Jung (1875-1961), *Symbols of Transformation*.

and the more belligerent gods were plied with ritual and sacrifice to appease them.

All of nature was alive. All things of the Earth, ocean, and sky had a voice with which they imparted grievances, warnings or joyous news. Man was one of those voices and the gods were speaking through him.

Ancient man knelt before many altars, he had many gods, and today those gods peek out at us from fable and myth.

All gods and goddesses found their way into man's life through a need or through an unusual experience. "These supernatural images were given," according to C.G. Jung (*Symbols of Transformation*) "characters that distinguish them from other forms of being." Many of our mythical gods come to us as half man and half beast—or bird. In Egyptian myths, Horus, the son of Osiris and Isis, is pictured with the head of a hawk, a bird man sometimes with the name Iusa. Horus is, in Egyptian myth, the god that is reborn every twenty-five thousand years so that he might descend to Earth and help its humans. Vera Stanley Alder tells us (*Finding of the Third Eye*):

> The ancient civilizations of the Near East were familiar with a sun worship dominated by the idea of the dying and resurgent god...

The Hopi have the Kachina People who come to Earth, taking human form, leading them and teaching them how to survive. Many of the different cultures bowed down to similar gods. For instance, in Egyptian mythology the god Thoth is given the position of creator god but later is found in the office of advanced education, being portrayed as Aah, the moon god, wearing a crescent and lunar disk. However, in Greek mythology the god Thoth takes on the name of Hermes, and becomes a messenger for all the gods, being pictured with winged heels. His other positions include god of science, commerce, eloquence, cunning, and god of those souls departing to Hades. Later he becomes Hermes Trismegistus, the mythical founder of alchemy and other occult sciences.

The mythologies of the Americas range from the deification of the Totem to the spiritually evolved cultures of the Incas, the Mayans, and the Aztecs.

Great Spirit, Earth Mother, Coyote (or Trickster), are prominent in the myths of most tribes. The worship of the sun was, at one time, an important part of the Aztec and Mayan rites. In Christianity, Mohammedanism, and Judaism, God has been defined in accordance with the tenets of those creeds.

In our Western culture we have nourished many beliefs: Monotheism pays homage to only one God; Polytheism relies spiritually on many gods, which seem to be thought of as different manifestations of a single God. Deism pays reverence to a remote Creator, and Theism enshrines a personal God who is hard at work within the precincts of His own world. Pantheism carries the assurance that everything has its being in a God and that God is a part of all creations, and Panentheism persuades us that God is identical with the universe.

But in the world that man created around the religious beliefs, the gods became more and more like the humans that bowed down to them. With the complexities of an ever evolving society man became faced with increasing demands on his canonical convictions. During those unstable times old gods were sometimes traded for the new who would serve the needs better. At other stages, with a little fence mending, older gods were stylized to fit the new economic and political framework. And it was often true that man and his gods were significantly altered by military invasions that whisked their way through countries previously divorced from one another by boundaries, language, and customs. About the same time that the Israelites emigrated from Egypt to Canaan, Ionians, Achaeans, and Dorians were pouring into Greece. The conquerors found various religions flourishing in the different parts of Greece. All were emotionally absorbed; the recipients placing them in a region of worship somewhere above or within the superstitions of the creative minds that had brought these gods, and perhaps their miracles, into existence. Many times the ultimate acceptance of Christianity's God was the result of political prudence.

What has been contemptuously termed Paganism was really ancient wisdom replete with Deity. Judaism, Christianity, and the Islamic scriptures have derived whatever spiritual inspiration they possess from this heathen parent. Pre-Vedic Brahmanism and Buddhism are the double source from which all religions were born. It is quite apparent that the many religious beliefs that mankind have professed all down through history have all had their origin in the same primitive source. According to Jung *(Symbols of Transformation)*:

> 'God' is the name for a complex of ideas grouped round a powerful feeling....man, in consequence, worships the psychic force active within him as something divine.

In all ages the gods have been consigned to the role of men. There are tombs designating the burial spots of Zeus, Hercules, and Bacchus, expressing their mortality. They were, back in ancient times, a part of life on Earth. But the human could not conceptualize their heroes as confined to the mortal struggle on Earth. These larger-than-life entities must reside above their human charges in a place of light and beauty. The residence of all the gods was Heaven. There, they laughed, they played, they made love, and in some cultures, even war. And the small human was finding that even with great sacrifices such as prize animals and strong tribal heroes laid on their altars, their gods might fail to respond. They were too busy to hear the pleas of the insignificant Earth-man. To fill their need for satisfying dialogue with the gods, creative minds gave birth to spiritual messengers, the Angels.

Our Biblical "Angels," celestial representatives who descended to Earth from "Heaven Overhead," according to the readings of Edgar Cayce (*Destiny of Man*, by Lytle Robinson), were those Angels that were given food by Lot:

> ...and he took butter and milk and the calf which he had dressed and set it before them; and he stood by them under the tree and they did eat. (Gen. 18:4-58).

And there were the "sons of God" who saw the daughters of men, "and they were fair." And those gods intermarried with the fair humans and created demi-gods who would rule over Earth.

From the Westcar Papyrus we hear this:

> Ra came down from heaven and was united with Ruttett, the wife of a priest of the god Ra, from this union came Sahura and Kakaa. Every king of Egypt was an offspring of this union.

27

Cayce tells us:

> ...Amilius himself descended into matter and
> became Adam...the first of the perfect race, the
> first of the Sons of God as opposed to
> Daughters of Man, the freakish offspring of
> the Mixtures.

And there are stories of men mating with animals, out of
which came weird creatures, giants, chimeras, and man.
Cayce tells us:

> ...the monstrosities roamed the earth and
> mixed with the animals. Sex was the
> determining factor.

The monstrosities that we find in our myths include
one-eyed cyclops, giants[2], sea serpents, mermaids, and
mermen, Circe, Homer's enchantress who turned men into
swine, and fire-spouting dragons. The Chi'Wara, a
mythical half man half beast is credited in the Bambara
society[3] of Mali as being the ancient teacher responsible
for their present farming system.

Priests of the Dogon tribe talk about a time when the
gods came regularly to play on Earth and they worship a
pyramid with a square platform at the top where, they
claim, the sky gods landed long, long ago.[4] And from
Andre Tomas (*On the Shores of Endless Worlds*) we hear:

---

[2] "... King Og of Bashan was the last of the giant Rephaim." (*Holy
Bible, King James Version,* Deuteronomy 3:11). His iron bedstead
is kept in a museum at Rabbak one of the cities of the
Ammonites, it measures thirteen and a half feet long by six feet
wide.

[3] Inhabitants of the Bandeogara Plateau in the West African
Republic.

[4] *Mysteries of the Unexplained,* Readers Digest Association, Inc.
1982.

Herodotus was informed by the initiated priesthood, that the descent of the sky gods had taken place in 17,500 B.C., and that this traffic continued until 11,850 B.C., after which no god ever assumed mortal form.

A recognition of Star People runs through all of our ancient myths. From the *Bible* (King James Version) we hear of Angels that mysteriously appear. From the *Book of Ezekiel* (1:4):

As I looked, behold, a stormy wind came out of the north, and a great cloud, with brightness round about it—and when the living Creatures rose from the earth, the wheels rose. (*Holy Bible,* King James Version)

Ancient Indian legends claim that the Star Gods came in fiery chariots and built Tiahuanaco, the "Celestial City." Peru has the god Virachoca rising out of Lake Titicaca, riding through the sky, leaving a geological division of mountains and valleys before he disappeared in the sky like a "flaring comet."

We hear this from the Hebraic writings (The Old Testament), according to Sitchin (*The Stairway to Heaven*):

They were the Mighty Ones of Eternity, the People of the Shem, the People of the Rocketships...Nefilim (giants), 'Those Who Were Cast Upon' the earth.

The Nefilim were upon the Earth in those days and thereafter too.

It was some 450,000 years ago, the Sumerian texts claim, that astronauts from Marduk came to Earth in search of gold. Not for jewelry, but for some pressing need affecting survival on the Twelfth Planet...[5]

Fifty astronauts, they were called Anunnaki—Those of Heaven Who Are on Earth—splashed down in the Arabian Sea. Their commander was a brilliant scientist and engineer. His hobbies were sailing the seas and fishing so he was given the name of E.A.—He Whose House is Water. He was the first son of Anu, god of Marduk—He of The Heavens, and like all Sumerian gods his distinguishing feature was the horned headdress.

Ancient texts tell us that the days before the "Deluge" were the days when "The Nefilim" (Genesis 6) were upon the Earth. Zecharia Sitchin (*The Stairway to Heaven*) claims that: "Biblical tales of the Creation and the events leading to the Deluge are condensed Hebrew versions of Sumerian traditions." And the biblical term "Watchers" used to classify the sons of gods is the same as that used by the Egyptians. And Watchers is the exact meaning of the name Shumer, the god's landing place on Earth.

Edgar Cayce (*Destiny of Man*, by Lytle Robinson) describes Earth at the time of man's beginning:

> ...the Garden of Eden (was) in that land which lies now much in the desert, yet much in the mountain and much in the rolling lands there. The extreme northern portions were then the southern. The polar regions were then turned to where they occupied more of the tropical

---

[5]According to Sumerian beliefs, it was from the Twelfth Planet, the twelfth member of the solar system, that astronauts had come to Earth. These gods created mankind and its civilization. In myth, the twelfth planet is referred to as Marduk, a planet from outer space which was drawn into the solar system. Zecharia Sitchin, *The Stairway to Heaven.*

and semi-tropical regions....The Nile entered into the Atlantic Ocean.

What is now the Sahara was an inhabited land and very fertile. What is now the central portion of this country, or the Mississippi basin, was then all in the ocean; only the plateau was existent, or the regions that are now portions of Nevada, Utah and Arizona formed the greater part of what we know as the United States. That along the Atlantic Seaboard formed the outer portion then, or the lowlands of Atlantis. The Andeans, or the Pacific coast of South America, occupied then the extreme western portion of Lemuria. The Urals and the northern regions of same were turned into a tropical land. The desert in the Mongolian land was then the fertile portion....

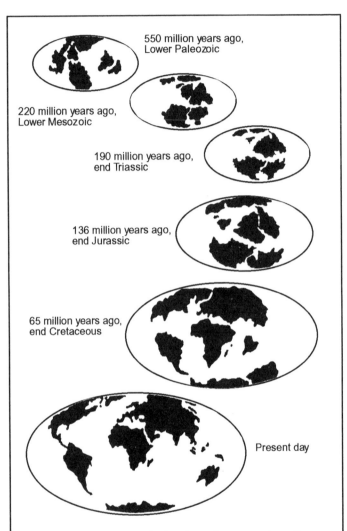

550 million years ago,
Lower Paleozoic

220 million years ago,
Lower Mesozoic

190 million years ago,
end Triassic

136 million years ago,
end Jurassic

65 million years ago,
end Cretaceous

Present day

This series of maps traces the breakup of supercontinent Pangaea.
It was formed by the collision of primordial continents some 250
million years ago. It then split into two continents, southern
Gondwanaland and northern Laurasia. Further fragmentation
yielded continents as we know them today.

3
THE EARTH

> Because of the dynamism of the Earth and the many changes that have affected its surface since its creation, the oldest rocks we find are about 3.5 billion years old. These are found in Greenland and South Africa. This means that the first billion years of Earth's history have been obliterated. (Robert M. Powers, *Planetary Encounters*)

We believe that the Earth is a huge magnet with a north and south magnetic pole, differing from the geographical pole with, according to my Random House dictionary, the distinction of being the "region of a magnet towards which the lines of induction converge (south), and diverge (north)." The geographical poles are, very simply, part of our present geography. Our scientists will agree on this. But those of that faction of science who study our Earth cannot seem to agree on why the Earth is a huge magnet and the reason for the magnetic changes. This mysterious force that seems to generate somewhere around a theorized hard metal core goes through periodic changes and the magnetic poles shift slowly but constantly.

Through the eyes of an astronomer our Earth-world takes on the appearance of a very small speck in a vast universe of millions of similar bright specks. One hundred thousand million stars make up the dish-like disk that is the galaxy of which Earth is a very small part and which John Gribbon (*Genesis: The Origin of Man and the Universe*) describes as looking like "a huge Catherine wheel of stars with a central bulge some seven kiloparsecs[1] across surrounded by tightly wrapped spiral arms covering a total diameter of some thirty kiloparsecs." Each star performs at its own speed as it tracks the center of the Milky Way. The speed depends on the individual distance from the center. There is a constant birthing of new stars, forming in loose clusters and more than seven hundred of these clusters are found in the immediate vicinity of Earth's solar system. But, we are told:

In the beginning, billions of years ago, the universe was a blank space of darkness. Matter was a thin mist of nothing. Yet everything that was there—the darkness and the nothing—would, in a long flight of time, move, and twirl restlessly into a universe—or universes—of planets and solar systems.

The Book of the Hopi (Frank Waters and Oswald White Bear Fredericks) makes the statement that before the First World, Topela by name,

> ...there was only the Creator, Taiowa. All else was endless space....Just an immeasurable void that had its beginning and end...in the mind of Taiowa....Sotuknang, following Taiowa's instructions created the universe. On the earth air, water and mountains were brought into being.

Hinduism carries the belief that the universe had no absolute beginning and likewise will have no absolute ending. Man first appeared in India, based on archeological finds, between 400,000 and 200,000 B.C.

---

[1] One kiloparsec is one thousand parsecs or 3,260 light years.

Jewish tradition dates the Creation at 3761 B.C. and the Bible tells it this way (Genesis 1:2, *Holy Bible,* King James Version):

> And the earth was without form, and void; darkness was upon the face of the deep. And the Spirit of God moved upon the face of the waters.

Adrian Clark, a space engineer, tells us in *Cosmic Mysteries of the Universe,* "...which could not be H_2O, the type of water we now know, if there was no earth."

In Eckankar, Paul Twitchell conceptualizes our beginning based on Hindu religious principles:

> When God created the world, that is the lower worlds, and left them to the interest of the governments and the planetary spirits of these regions to run, he divided them into three distinct planes. The topmost is Brahmanda, the middle is Anda, and the last is Pinda the physical world.

From the readings of Edgar Cayce, a twentieth century prophet, as found in *Origin and Destiny of Man* by Lytle Robinson we hear:

> ...the Cosmos was built by and upon the principles which became known as music, arithmetic, and geometry; harmony, system and balance. By changing the rate of vibration...varying movements, patterns, forms and substances came into being....Each dimension had its own set of laws; the earth represents the third dimension, the testing laboratory for the entire system.

In the centuries that followed a new interpretation of the universe emerged. Determinism described the universe as a "huge clock" set in motion at the beginning of time and then left undisturbed to manage by itself. In this the presence of a single Divine engineer is seen.

A more modern approach is the one brought out by the McKennas (Terrence and Dennis, *The Invisible Landscape*) which is based on our recent scientific laser photography and sees our world as a hologram, "...created by the interaction of two lasers." One consequence of this they explain here:

> ...if our universe is a hologram, every part contains the information of the whole, as in normal photography.

This bit of interesting news on that subject came out of the *Miami Herald*, 1981:

> More than 25 years after their invention by man, the first laser occurring in nature has been discovered in the upper-atmosphere of Mars.

This falls, very neatly, under an ancient cliché: "As above, so below," the belief that Earth is merely a reflection of another more beautiful world. If our reality is an illusion, it is an illusion caused by a greater reality. And, of course, we have the more recent theory brought into being by the discoveries in quantum mechanics. Here, in *Science Digest* (Aug., 1986), Michael Deering Lemonick explains it:

> One of the apparently nonsensical dictums of the reigning school of quantum theory is that the observer creates the phenomenon observed....Our existence as observers is a neces-

sary prerequisite to the existence of everything else.

Is man the Creator of Earth? Lemonick continues, quoting David Hume, Scottish philosopher (1711-1776):

> The most that a man who accepts it is entitled to conclude is that the universe, sometime, arose from something like design. But beyond this position he cannot ascertain one single circumstance, and is left afterwards to fix every point of his theology, by the utmost license of fancy and hypothesis.

What do we actually know about Earth? Cosmologists do not agree on when the universe began. Eric J. Lenner says in *Discover* (June issue, 1988):

> The Big Bang Never Happened....In the Big Bang, a crucial assumption is that gravity is the dominant force in the shaping of the cosmos. Another is that...the distribution of matter on the large scale is everywhere the same....But now it appears...huge aggregates of matter...span a billion light years or more....These observations conflict with all current versions of the Big Bang theory.

The most widely held theory of the planets is that of a formation through cosmic elements such as hydrogen, oxygen, nitrogen, and carbon from universally distributed materials present in a primitive atmosphere. The earliest form is thought to be water, ammonia, methane, and hydrogen. Out of this, we did believe, came our lithosphere, troposphere, tropopause, stratosphere, and hydrosphere, all part of an atmosphere, a protective gaseous net that is appraised by some cosmologists as the creation of a Master Builder.

That scientifically structured protective net does not respond to man's theory of evolution, the evolving of a universal world out of a spontaneous heavenly explosion. The designer of those precise gaseous layers, say our men of science, had to have a Ph.D. in physics, a masters in engineering, and a fantastic imagination.

EARTH'S ATMOSPHERE

We are told that the atmosphere weighs about fifteen pounds per square inch. In the troposphere—the lower layer of atmosphere—the temperature drops steadily. At seven miles up from this lower layer, there are high winds known as the jetstream, which move at a speed up to 500 miles an hour. One mile further up from the jet-stream all is calm and this remains constant through the stratosphere—the upper layer of the atmosphere. Ten miles beyond the stratosphere the temperature rises; here there is no protection against the sun's destructive ultra-violet rays. Seventy miles above the Earth there is an ionized layer of atmosphere that reflects radio waves back to Earth, and 1,500 miles above Earth we find the magnetosphere—the Van Allen Belt—from which dangerous radioactivity extends for thousands of miles into space.

Information coming out of that field of science tells us that most of the weather and climate processes occur in the troposphere but the atmosphere shields the Earth and is the only gas which absorbs ultra-violet radiation. We also hear that the evolution of the lithosphere, hydrosphere and atmosphere have been strongly influenced by the biosphere—the sphere of living things—our Earth.

Today our science tells us that the only thing keeping Earth from meteoric destruction in our present time is the atmosphere, that gaseous net which extends to a height of

22,000 miles and rotates with the Earth, and cannot be seen—even by scientists —as a product of evolution. More, it is analyzed by some as a "biological invention," as in *The Star Thrower* by Loren Eiseley:

> ...that single invention, for such it was determined, is responsible for the entire nature of life on this planet, and there is no possibility of calling it preordained.

And this from the *Great World Atlas*:

> Earth's atmosphere, the blanket of gases surrounding the planet is the factor that more than any other, enables us to exist.

An estimate given by the Harvard Observatory makes the statement that over 100,000,000,000 (100 billion) meteors penetrate our atmosphere every twenty-four hours and out of that number no more than thirty ever reaches Earth in a twenty-four hour period. And these are in a much reduced condition.

This from Colin Wilson (*Starseeker*):

> The total effect of this layer of air is to provide the earth with a cushion of tremendous stopping power. The air we breathe is the most efficient armor conceivable. In mass it is equivalent to a thickness of fifty-two inches of the toughest steel armor plate.

There is a constant atmospheric activity. But below we also have many interesting things going on as part of Earth's surface life. And many of these are as mysterious and questionable as those of space.

EARTH'S CONSTRUCTION

We know very little about Earth aside from its surface which we are constantly trying to evaluate and measure. The interior of Earth is known to us only through the recording of vibrations. Shockwaves. The waves move slowly through the high density material and more quickly through lighter substances. These vibrations "bounce" back from the different levels giving scientists a rather vague theory as to the composition of Earth's interior. We are still asking the same questions in the day of modern science: What caused the different magnetic fields that we find in the rock strata? How did these magnetic fields originate? Are the mountains a record of cataclysmic history or one of gradual growth? How do we explain the layers of water—warm, cold, salt, and fresh—that move together in the oceans of our world? And one that comes out of our Big Bang theory: Is the center of our Earth really a ball of glowing hot metal?

We know from our current and past history that at least part of Earth's interior is hot enough to melt rock and send rivers of flowing lava over vast tracts of land and water, building new worlds. But we have to ask: Is all the interior that temperature? And if so, was this always the case? Are these extreme temperatures the result of a cooling planet? Or here is a question that might come out of our modern science—are these extreme temperatures caused by a runaway meltdown from a chain of nuclear reactors placed there at the time of Earth's construction?

Geologists tell us that we are riding giant conveyor belts floating on top of a molten mantle of rocks, carrying formations of land with them. This is the way Rick Gore ("Our Restless Earth," National Geographic) describes it:

> Seven major plates and many minor plates:
> slabs of rigid rock averaging 100 kilometers
> (60 miles) thick that ride like icebergs in a
> more fluid layer of hot rock below....

A. Mohorovocic, a Yugoslavian geologist, searching for answers to the questions on the construction of inner Earth instigated the Mohole project. A deep-sea drilling operation. The intention was to drill into and past Earth's crust, penetrating the mantle and, hopefully, bring to the surface for close examination, samples of the mantle and the core. But the project had to be abandoned when it became apparent that beneath the crust lay an impenetrable shell, since labeled Earthshield and discussed as the "Mohorovocic Discontinuity." The shield lay at different depths, 125,000 feet under the continents and 15,000 to 20,000 feet beneath the ocean floors. N. J. Berrill (*Worlds Without End*) asks these interesting questions:

> How mobile is the immensely thick mantle?
> Do convection currents in the stony surface
> cause the continental masses in the crust to
> slide about?

Alfred Wegener, professor of geophysics and meteorology at the University of Graz, Austria, developed the theory of continental drift to explain the changes in the land formations. The continents, according to professor Wegener, began to break up in the Mesozoic Era. The mythical continent of Atlantis can be seen, in this theory, as North America after Atlantis had shifted positions. Wegener believes that there were a number of episodes of extreme repositioning.

Immanuel Velikovsky (*Earth in Upheaval*) tells us that what now is the Sahara Desert was once a fertile pasture land surrounding a great lake. The change came through a cataclysmic upheaval.

In addition to the violent wrenchings of Earth's crust, we have to deal with other oddities which do not conform to the image we have of our world.

For instance, archeologists are now describing North America some 10,000,000 (ten million) years ago as being a tropical savannah where herds of animals such as camels, zebras and rhinoceros made their home. The skeletal remains found in the southeastern part of the United States are believed to be the result of a huge volcanic eruption.

And in company with Earth's catastrophes, or perhaps guiding it, we have uncovered another of Earth's strange features: those electro bands—the magnetic paths, electromagnetic tracks, that are today being acknowledged by Russian scientists in technical papers as "a crystal shaped grid that underlies the surface of the world, and whose intersection points mark significant places in Earth's history," (as quoted in *Earth Magic* by Francis Hitching). This comes from Swedish Nobel Laureate, Hannes Alfren:

> ...the universe is crisscrossed and sculpted by titanic electric currents and vast magnetic fields.... The universe is ninety-nine percent plasma—ionized gas that can conduct electricity.

Probes that were made in the 1960s have shown that Alfren's theory is right. Currents and magnetic filaments are now known to exist throughout the solar system.

"Since early times," says Francis Hitching (*Earth Magic*), "there has been a belief in the existence of natural leys, bands of force two or three yards wide, extending twenty to thirty feet above and below the surface of the earth." And a Rhode Island electrical engineer believes that he has detected and recorded electromagnetic anomalies on the path of the leys.

Oceanographers of the National Oceanic and Atmosphere Administration have recently discovered that there is a "very close fit between the 1,000 fathom lines of the coast of North America and North Africa if Cape Hatteras is linked to Cape Verde." Here Melchoir Newmayr and Eduard Suess (*The Face of the Earth*) speculate about the shifting of continents:

> During the Jurassic and Cretaceous Periods when dinosaurs ruled the world, there was one large continent in the Southern Hemisphere, Godwana-land... at the same time, there were two continents in the Northern Hemisphere, Godwana-land gradually broke up by the sinking of various parts....

In 1913 an American, Marshall B. Gardner, published a book in which he set out to prove that the Sun was not above the Earth, but inside it. The pressure exerted by the rays, in this theory, kept the human population attached to the Earth's surface. However, the Vril secret society claim beings endowed with superior powers inhabit the center of the Earth and one day will reign over humanity.

But there have always been, and I trust always will be, the dreamers who prefer to find beneath that impassable shield, secreted away from the eyes of society, a mysterious world. An unfathomable territory peopled in myth and legend by devils and gods; giants, gnomes, trolls, elves and The Little People. A hollow Earth, open only to fools, children, and the imagination of inquiring minds. In European folk-lore dragons make their home underground, and in Japan, legend tells of a monster dwelling deep beneath their island that is responsible for earthquakes.

There are those today who speak of and believe in the polar regions as openings leading to a vast underground space. And there are those among them who make the claim that the news of a discovered hollow Earth is being suppressed by governments to prevent the exploration of that inner world.

Although it might be easier for some among us—who do not have the creative imagination to deal with it—to dismiss such reports as the ravings of a few lunatics, still, it is interesting to note that more than a few old documents, ancient writings, including the scriptures, allude to an inner world. For instance: from the *Hebrew Book of Light*, 12th-13th century: "There were men from the sky in the Earth in those days." And we have been told to believe that Gilgamesh, the Sumerian king and great hero, went down into "the bowels of the Earth," seeking immortality from his ancestor Atnapishtim. And it was in that Inner World that Orpheus sought the soul of Euridice. Ulysses offered up sacrifices to induce the Ancient Ones to "rise up from the depths of the Earth" and give him advice.

The Mongols of Russia have legends and beliefs dealing with the gods who are said to come from the center of the Earth. And Hindu books speak of god-like emissaries coming from inner Earth in flying ships. Doctor Lobsang Rampa (*Twilight*), a Tibetan lama, gives this answer to the question of inner worlds:

> ...the religion...in which I am the most informed does indeed refer to an Inner World....
> It is called "Agharta"... in the Tibetan lore there is much mention made of Shamballa,

where the King of all the world lives, the King who is hidden from the millions on the surface of the world...there are tunnels in Tibet that go deeper and deeper... and there are legends about strange people coming up through those tunnels, holding converse with lamas of high degrees.

Doctor Rampa tells us there are also tunnels between Brazil and the inner world:

Brazil and Tibet are two vitally important parts of the outer world which have a special attraction for the Inner People.

Erich Von Daniken (*Gold of the Gods*), gives us a current find, a tunnel system in South America. This is the way he describes it:

... a gigantic system of tunnels thousands of miles in length... lies hidden deep below the South American continent. Hundreds of miles of underground passages have already been explored and measured in Ecuador and Peru....

There are many reports on discovered caves and tunnels running like super highways beneath those that we "upstairs" inhabitants follow around our surface world. Many caves and tunnels have been discovered beneath the Caucasus. One large tunnel led to a spacious underground hall more than sixty-five feet high. The Tibetans believe that the creators of these tunnels were "Beings that live near the stars."[2]

---

[2] "The thing under Ellesmere Island begins about 15 miles beneath the Earth's surface and drops to a depth of at least 80 miles. It seems to extend across the boundary of the Earth's mantle crust."(*Gods, Demons & Space Chariots*, Eric Norman)

There are persistent legends within most cultures that tell of the Ancient Ones or the Old Ones. According to one writer, Brad Steiger (*Atlantis Rising*), we hear: "In virtually all the legends, the Old Ones have gone underground to escape natural catastrophes or the hidden death that exists in the life-giving rays of our sun. These Old Ones are the teachers from the caves," he tells us.

Doctor Roger Wescott sees the Cave Masters as spacemen who "grew disgusted with *Homo Sapiens* and retreated to underneath bases from which they might watch over the primitive species...." And at times they would walk among those surface dwellers offering advice.

The theory of a hollow Earth has been kept alive by those of the human race who were not afraid to think their way into Earth's mysterious underground world. There were the science fictionists who found it, and left it—a wildly unpredictable, totally enjoyable, and quite lucrative journey of the imagination.

Jules Verne, the author of that mind-bender *A Journey to the Center of the Earth*, was a small boy when Edgar Allen Poe published his tale of that inner world, *The Narrative of Arthur Gordon Pym*, describing a fantastic land located at Earth's center and reached through an opening at the North Pole. These were considered entertainment for the young, and the wonderful stories told first by Edgar Allen Poe and later by Jules Verne could be found only on the bookshelves of children.

There were these dreamers, and then there was Captain Symms. In the early nineteenth century, America was introduced to the theory of the "hollow Earth" by a Captain Cleves Symms. Captain Symms asked the help of the United States Congress and the leading citizens of many other countries in financing an exploration into the interior of the Earth. In his correspondence with the different officials, Symms claimed to have proof that the interior of the Earth was made up of "several solid, concentric spheres placed one inside the other," and that they had openings at the poles. Needless to say, Captain Symms was labeled "crackpot" and ignored. But the fascination with an inner world did not go away. It came to light again with Hitler's rise to power and his obsession with the doctrine of a Hollow Earth. But again, and this time because of Hitler's deserved reputation of "Madman," it was scornfully discarded along with those materials from other "cranks" and "fools."

Buddhist scriptures acknowledge stories of a mysterious land concealed within the depths of the Himalayas,[3] hidden away from the eyes and minds of the surface dwellers, a fabled Kingdom perhaps named Agharta. But pulling on the same thread of fantasy, we have reports coming out of the same sources that tell of a secreted underground empire, Shambala by name. And to further this Arabian Night's Tale, Hindu books speak of god-like emissaries who "come from inner earth in flying machines."

The theory of UFOs originating inside our Earth is set out by O. C. Huguenin in his work *From the Subterranean World to the Sky: Flying Saucers*. But apparently this conviction was initially put forward by Professor Henrique Jose Desouza, president of the Brazilian Theosophical Society. I find it interesting that the Theosophical Society is headquartered in Sao Laurenca, in the State of Minas Geiors, where there is a great temple dedicated to

---

[3]"The Nagas of India, known as the Flying Serpents, are believed to have built vast subterranean cities in the Himalayas," taken from *On the Shores of Endless Worlds* by Andre Tomas.

Aghartz, (Agharta?) the Buddhist word for subterranean world.

To add to the unusual picture of strange flying machines being quartered somewhere below our nicely manicured lawns, there is the enigma of unusual aircraft plummeting out of the sky, past non-believing observers, only to disappear in the depths of the waters, especially around the Bahamas. But according to reports, Lake Superior seems to be another port of entry into an underground hangar.

Here we might inquire: Are we to believe that beings alien to our civilization live in secret underwater bases and are monitoring—or directing—the lives of those living on the surface?

> "There is a hole in the sea through which ships disappear without a trace," says Robert Charoux (*Forgotten Worlds*).

Statistics coming out of Lloyds of London make the incredible claim that "Between 1929 and 1954, not counting the years of World War II, two hundred and twenty-two vessels disappeared in all the oceans of the world" and without leaving any evidence that they had ever existed.

Now we should want to know, are those inner Earth inhabitants responsible for all of Earth's disasters? The volcano eruptions and earth quakes? Do these advanced beings have the power to influence what we call the "natural" forces of the cosmos? And do they initiate—and if so why—the destructive shifting of Earth's poles?

Doctor Jeffrey Goodman (*We Are the Earthquake Generation*) speaks of the apparent unstable condition of the axis spin as the result of earthquakes which could create a pole shift with the right triggering mechanism. And one such triggering device, he tells us, is a "celestial body passing close to the Earth."

Scientific findings indicate more than one change in the position of the poles,[4] and quite possibly due to just such a catastrophe. Peter Warlow, in an article in Britain's *Journal of Physics* in 1978, makes the statement that a near miss with one or more cosmic bodies "could make the Earth turn over." And he believes that a large number of pole reversals have taken place.

And from Immanuel Velikovsky (*Earth in Upheaval*) we hear this: "In all parts of the globe rock formations are found with reversed polarization."

According to Stanley Miller and Harold Urey at the University of Chicago, both Earth and its Moon were "constantly being blasted by comets and meteorites until about four billion years ago." And Joan Oro, chemist at the University of Houston, tells us: "As many as 100,000 comets may have hit the Earth during the first billion years of its history." Today our scientists are measuring the comets.

COMETS

One of the comets that flew across the sky in 1811 was found to be nearly fourteen miles across in the widest part, and measured 116 miles long. But a second one in that same year had a tail[5] that extended 140,000,000 (140

---

[4] The focal point of the magnetic pole moves around a 14,000 mile circle, 18 miles per year, the complete orbit taking approximately 235 years.

[5] When a comet comes close to the sun its bright blasts are repelled by the supergenerated energy of the sun and therefore the comet-generated energy is thrown back upon itself, curling

million) miles. If we accept this concept and visualize a body fifty times the size of our moon, and being thrown out of orbit by a collision with another cosmic body, we might envision a fearsome monster streaking across the heavens and heading, quite possibly, straight for Earth. Science tells us that the gases which make up a comet are highly combustible when mixed with oxygen. And we know that Earth is a planet composed largely of oxygen. So—what would happen when this comet met up with Earth? Fireworks! Probably the first and definitely the most incredible cosmic Chinese New Year exhibition ever staged.

According to ancient Earth records, myths, and legends, our world went through creation and destruction many times before it arrived at its present form. The Cabala tells of a whole series of worlds evolving out of chaos only to die and be reborn in another fashion. [6]

Edgar Cayce in a reading on Atlantis (5748-1, May 28,1925) gives us these dates as times of Earth catastrophes: 50,000 B.C., 28,000 B.C., and 10,000 B.C.

Doctor Velikovsky is one of a number who suggest that one of the catastrophes, an electro-magnetic field reversal, was the result of a collision between a comet and three planets, Earth, Mars, and Venus. And, in keeping with this information, those who support this theory claim

---

around the body of the comet, streaming out behind like a fantastic tail of pulsating colors.

[6] Writings on the great idol of Tiahuanoco record that a moon came into orbit around Earth between 11,000 and 13,000 years ago and was making 425 revolutions in a 288 day year, according to Professor Bellamy and Dr. P. Allan (*The Great Idol of Tiahuanaco*). This almost coincides with the theory of Hans Hoerbiger, Austrian engineer and cosmologist (1927).

there is evidence of a major encounter between Venus and a comet in 1450 B.C., with a similar encounter between Mars and a comet in the ninth century B.C.

And here, from MIT we have:

> Given the right combination of impactor mass and speed and an off-center hit, a giant impact could convey the right amount and angular momentum to create a "topsy-turvey" solar system such as we have. Mercury is tilted and moves in a squashed orbit, Earth rotates rapidly and at a tilt of 23.5 degrees, Venus hardly rotates at all, while Uranus is lying on its side, and Pluto is a small sphere in a wild orbit.

Scientists at MIT look at Earth's satellite as the end product of a collision between Earth and a smaller planet which became its Moon—an encounter brought on by a ricocheting comet. James Jones of the Johnson Space Center contends that, "the Moon's formation through a giant impact is a very attractive hypothesis."

But if we were to consider this type of meeting between Earth and its Moon as a logical operation, then we would quite naturally be asking about other planets and the other satellites that make up our galaxy. Was—or maybe is—this a generally accepted way of acquiring a working companion? Strictly by chance, we might ask? And in the next breath we would want to know what are the odds of this happening more than once? And to other planets in the galaxy? With the same results?

There are those in the Cosmic fields of science that view Earth's Moon as a part of a Big Bang explosion, theorizing that an erupting fragment of earth spewed out into space only to be caught in its ascension and held in position by Earth's gravity.

The picture generally accepted by most of today's humanity is one of a universal explosion that sent all galactic matter thundering out into space in all directions. The Big Bang theory postulates that the last of the heavenly bodies to evolve from that original cosmic explosion were the planets and their satellites, or moons.

But what happens to any or all of our hypothesized theories if we accept the evidence brought back by that new breed of explorer who walked upon our Moon?

Buzz Aldrin (*Return to Earth*) tells us, "Actually more of a small planet than a moon."

If we are to recognize our Moon as Earth's satellite, how do we explain the documented information that has come out of that Moon Mission?

Rocks recovered from the surface of the Moon have been dated at twenty billion years. And some were found to be of an entirely different composition from those on Earth. Rocks laying side by side differed in age, and it was determined by analysis that the lunar dust did not come from the Moon rocks. It was alien to any on the surface of the Moon.

And we have from Dr. Gordon McDonald, a leading scientist at the National Aeronautics and Space Administration, a published report in which Dr. McDonald makes the unusual observation that the Moon appears to be hollow (Dr. H.P. Wilkins, *Our Moon*). Two Soviet theorists are making the claim that the Moon has a hollow area within it, filled with gases of some kind, an atmosphere in which to sustain life.

Dr. Wilkins tells us that there is a vast system of caves hidden beneath the surface of our Moon and Dr. Gary Latham, a seismologist at NASA, claims that the crust of the Moon is at least twice as thick (about sixty kilometers) as the outer shell of any continent on Earth.

Those men of science who spend a great part of their waking hours peering through our huge modern telescopes, tracking celestial worlds, make the statement that strange things have been observed on the surface of our Moon. From the Director of the British Astronomical Association we hear of a mysterious bridge that spans twenty miles from one side to the other. And then there are the strange lunar domes, some as large as 700 feet in diameter. The Moon that moves poets and lovers is the subject of both science and myth. From the *Rig Veda, 1 adhyaya*[7]:

> Everyone who journeys out of this world goes
> to the Moon first—the Moon is the gateway to
> the celestial world and the man who can an-
> swer his questions, him he lets through.

Major Donald Keyhoe (*The Flying Saucer Conspiracy*) is of the opinion that extraterrestrials are on the Moon. He believes that "surface creatures" probably inhabited it before the atmosphere became too thin. Maybe there is a Man-in-the-Moon?

According to old legends there was a period in Earth's time when there was no Moon. All was darkness. And perhaps we should inquire: Does Earth need a Moon?

James Trefil, Robinson Professor of Physics, George Mason University, has made a discovery which makes us believe that in order for intelligent life to evolve, a planet

---

[7] Rig-Veda (rig'va'da) [sans, *Rigveda ric*, praise, hymn + veda, knowledge] the Veda of Verses (Psalms), the oldest and most important of the Hindu Vedas. The Veda is any of four ancient sacred books of Hinduism, consisting of chants, Psalms, etc., or considered collectively.

has to form in an orbit that, despite chaos, remains in the continuously habitable zone of its sun:

> Astronomers talk in terms of a "continuously habitable zone," a narrow band surrounding a star in which an orbiting planet can sustain liquid water on its surface for long periods of time.

And he tells us that Earth has never been outside of this zone. And he claims that Earth enjoys a stable axis rotation that the other planets in the "inner solar system" do not. "In fact, Mars' North Pole points all over the map," Trefil says:

> Earth's axis of rotation is an imaginary line that goes through the North and South poles. At the moment it is tilted at an angle of about 23.5 degrees from the vertical and describes a lazy circle in space every 26,000 years, much like the axis of a tilted spinning top. The amount of tilt doesn't change by more than a degree or so over geological periods of time. This means that many present features of Earth's climate— the alternations of seasons between summer and winter, for example—have always been present.

Then he adds that Earth is not only in an orbit that remains in a "continuously habitable zone of its sun," but Earth, unlike the other planets, has a moon that is large compared to itself. And it does appear accurate to say that the force the Moon exerts on the planet Earth serves to stabilize it, to control the axis of rotation of Earth. It seems that without the Moon, our own North Pole would "wobble around" like that of Mars. Apparently the Sun is not totally responsible for life on Earth as we once believed. In the past we were convinced that the planets circled in "a stately, repeating ellipse," Wisdom from MIT tells us, "just like clockwork. But that was when there was the solid belief that the Sun was responsible for all of this." There are new "facts," according to James Trefil, that tell us "the Sun is not the whole story." God has not wound up the clock. Now there is the belief that in order for intelligent life to evolve, a planet has to form in an orbit that remains in a continuously habitable zone; but in addition, perhaps that planet has to have a large moon.

James Trefil does suggest that Earth, based on its random acquisition of a supportive size moon could quite possibly be the only planet in the universe capable of sustaining intelligent life. G. I. Gurdjieff tells us: "From a cosmic point of view, Earth is cold and hard," and everything that man needs or wants he must struggle for. "Things that might come easily in another place must be fought for" (*The Story of Gurdjieff's Teachings,* Kenneth Walker).

Earth seen through the mind of Edgar Cayce is a laboratory, a testing ground for all universal life. Looking at it this way we might be inclined to see our planet not as the only one capable of sustaining life, but as the only world with the necessary requirements for the birth and evolution of a new life-form—humanity, an Experimental Probationary Cosmic Depot (EPCD). And as Gurdjieff sees it, the struggle is part of the evolution. Another thought here, from Barrows and Silk (*The Left Hand of Creation*):

> In many ways the universe seems tailor-made for life. It is cool enough, old enough and stable enough to evolve and sustain the fragile biochemistry of life.... It almost appears designed for the emergence of Man.

If we take into consideration Earth's construction "that thick mobile mantle; Earth's definite and constant orbit around the sun, never deviating, and those strange electrobands that run beneath the surface forming a net-like grid," it does smack of engineering of a most advanced type. This all builds up to an unwavering certainty in the mind of this author, that Earth was a deliberate fabrication and for a special purpose. The Beginning of Man? Or—a new world for a species whose plane of existence had been destroyed by fire, wind, and water?

There are as many different beliefs concerning the creation of man and his world as there are those looking for answers. To someone with a religious conception of the "Beginning" in the western sense, the word "Creation" will quite naturally be associated with God. For the follower of the Vedantic philosophy the same world will be one of illusion, termed Maya. Those in theosophy will deal with different planes, the physical world, the astral world, and so on. A physicist knows only the structures in matter while the astronomer sees a universe of ever-moving forms; a constant cycle of birthing and dying in space with no beginning and no end. Philosophy has its own interpretation and out of the mind of Jorge Luis Borges (*Other Inquisitions*) we hear this:

> We (that individual divinity that operates in us) have dreamed the world. We have dreamed it as enduring, mysterious, visible, omnipresent in space and stable in time.

From Sumerian texts quoted by Sitchin (*The Stairway to Heaven*, VI, 97) dating back to the fourth millennium B.C. we have this account in the words of the author:

> It was then that a large planet appeared from outer space and was drawn into the solar

56

system. The Sumerians called the invader NIBIRU— "Planet of the crossing." The Babylonian name for it was Marduk. As it passed by the outer planets Marduk's course curved into a collision course with an old member of the solar system—a planet named Tiamat. As the two came together the satellites of Marduk split Tiamat in half. Its lower part was smashed into bits and pieces, creating the comets and the asteroid belt—the "celestial bracelet," planetary debris that orbits between Jupiter and Mars. Tiamat's upper part, together with its chief satellite, were thrown into a new orbit to become Earth and its Moon.

Maybe that unfortunate meeting between Marduk and the planet Tiamat was the first of the many catastrophes that are a part of the history of our solar system. And perhaps tenants of Marduk were the gods that descended to Earth and delivered man from the mud and-water—the darkness of destruction. This comes from an old Chinese legend (*Beginnings: Earth, Sky, Life and Death,* Sophia Lyons Fahs and Dorothy T. Spoerl):

> Still the wonders grew that P'an Ku brought to pass.

Sitchin tells us that when Marduk invaded our solar system it brought with it the seed of life. During the collision some of this seed was transferred to the remaining half of Tiamat, planet Earth. And the evolution of life on Earth emulated the evolution of life on Marduk. But when life on Earth was just beginning to stir, life on Marduk had already reached high levels of civilization and technology. This, of course, would tend to foster the belief that Earth's human is related to the gods.

The oldest nations of the New World, Mayan, Aztec, and Inca, share, within their individual histories and legends, similar beliefs concerning the destruction of previous worlds. The Incas believed that after the creation by the god Wira Kocha, one of their civilizations was almost wiped out by a great flood which this god had sent to punish the first men. Only a few people were preserved to repopulate the world. When the flood had subsided, Wira Kocha suddenly appeared on Titicaca, he restored man's world, he gave them light. Out of *Revelation* (6:12-14) (*Holy Bible,* King James Version) we have:

> ...I saw a new heaven and a new earth, for the heaven and the first earth were passed away....

Immanuel Velikovsky (*Worlds in Collision*) tells us that Earth has been turned around more than once. The *Tractate Sanhedrin*[8] of the Talmud gives the name Tivel to a world in which the sun rose in the west. Harakte is the Egyptian name for that same world that the Koran describes as two easts and two wests.

Sacred Hindu writings from 200 B.C., (*Bhagavata Purana*)[9] lay claim to knowledge of four ages that came through damning events in which mankind was almost completely destroyed. From Toltec legends we hear:

> There was a tremendous hurricane that carried away trees, mounds, houses, and the largest edifices, notwithstanding which many men and women escaped, principally in caves and places where the hurricane could not reach them.

---

[8] Writings or discussions of the Sanhedrin, the Jewish nation's highest court which was destroyed in 70 A.D.
[9] Immanuel Velikovsky, (*Worlds in* Collision).

The *Zendavesta*[10] of the early Persians describes seven world ages. "Seven earths and seven heavens were created before ours," say early Hebrew documents.

Traditionally, the Polynesians claim nine successive worlds, each with a different sky above the earth. The Icelanders also carry a history of nine different worlds. In their *Poetic Edda* (translated by H.A. Bellows) they describe one destruction this way:

> With the death of Baldur came the twilight of the Gods. Time swept away the old gods and the giants in one last battle with Loki and his powers. But Loki too was destroyed. The ramparts of Asgard fell, worlds crashed in ruin, and the universe was no more. But out of the chaos and dark night a new heaven and a new earth were born.

---

[10] The sacred writings of the Zoroastrians quoted by Immanuel Velikovsky, (*Worlds in* Collision).

A Myth - *From the Mind of the Author:*

It is said, they moved above—below—and around it, knowing the smallest and the greatest of the complexities of this world these gods were about creating.

This new world hung like a giant thing, suspended in the air by no seen ropes, held only by the thought of these mighty gods.

If the minds of you that swallow each word that drops from my tongue would aspire to such a greatness you should see this can be so.

This new world now hung between one called Mars and the "Planet of death" which was waiting for a bright union with the all powerful—One, the fiery lord of the Heaven. The "Planet of death" was at this time at war with One, and being of inferior forces was slowly being overcome.

In our legends, it is acclaimed as the reason for the new world—which we are now a part of. Within this world, now hidden away from all but the eyes of the gods, are great cities, with never a shadow of darkness upon them. I have been told that the gods are of great stature. And I feel it must be so—for that world, of which we know nothing, but hear many things, must be of a higher nature.

Do your ears lend themselves to my words? And is it such that those ears and the good neighbor, mind, do understand one another? If that is the way of it I will find the path that will pass behind the eye, into this new world as it moves slowly, ever circling that mighty lord of the heaven—One. But, ever softly it steals around—so as not to disturb the livid monster whose red eyes set greedily upon the "Planet of death."

The Earth

I can see—you must know about these gods that did dwell between an earth and a sky, within this new world. And you ask, were they our g3ods—are we their children? They must look upon us this way—as far back as legends go, it has been said they were the wise men. The fathers, the teachers of man. But that must be told as it came about.

It is said that this unhappy earth was, in the beginning, a great paradise; but in the beginning, before the beginning of man, it was a great barren thing, moving around itself as it stayed upon the path of the smiling sun. But that Lord of the heavens has many faces and you must remember he has never closed his hungry eyes—he was ever watchful toward "dying planet"—and this caused much watchfulness on the part of Man.

Over the nearby dunes
Over the dunes afar
Our steps move together
Our isles are travelers

Then the wind
Sweeps the vast sands of the world
Scattering my images
Scattering my song

But I remain eternal
I leave, still I am
With other eyes
And other faces

And I look
On the nearby isles
On the isles afar
At the rose couries
on a white little beach
At the graceful wave
which flows from life to life
At the beautiful unending story

By the Body of the Earth, by Satprem,
translated from the French by Mariana Fitzpatrick

4
MAN

man 1 (man), n, pl.men, v., manned, manning.—
n. l. an adult male person, as distinguished from a
boy or woman. 2. an individual, Homo sapiens, at
the highest level of animal development, charac-
terized esp. by a highly developed brain and the
ability to reason abstractly and form articulate
speech. 3. the human individual as representing
the species; the human race; mankind. Ho-mo sa-
pi-ens (ho/mo/sa pe anz). *Random House Dictionary of the English Language*

Man, as seen in the medical model, is an incorporation
of head, trunk, arms, legs, fingers and toes. Medically we are
always interested in what makes these different parts operate
automatically. Man is, generally speaking, a conglomeration
of very efficient systems: circulatory, respiratory, digestive,
and that intricate bit of wiring called the nervous system.
And let us not forget those ambitious and undeniably mechanical scanning and alarm functions that are known as the
sensory system.

Here are a few more interesting facts. A three quarter
inch square of skin taken from the back of the hand contains
nine feet of blood vessels, thirty hair follicles, 84 oil glands,
300 sweat glands, 600 pain sensors, 36 heat sensors, 75 pressure sensors, 9,000 nerve endings and thirteen yards of
nerves.

Bones are twenty-five per cent water, forty-five per cent
minerals (mostly calcium): the other thirty per cent is comprised of living tissue, blood vessels and cells. About half
the bones of man's body are located in the hands and feet.

And, of course, we should be cognizant of the fact that each adult carries around in that matured body approximately five quarts of blood. All of this along with one heart, one pair of eyes, two ears, one mouth, two arms and two legs—complete with hands and feet, fingers, toes and thirty-two teeth make up one adult body - person - human - man - woman member of the human race, Homo Sapiens. Humanity. But we do not know why. Or how. Or when. The only reason we can go into all of this and talk about the possibility of understanding it is that we also possess that analyzing, dictator-instructor-collaborator, the brain, without which we probably would not be the least bit interested in any of this.

"To understand the brain, the heart, etc., they have to understand the mathematics of chaos," says Paul Rapp ("Chaotic Body," *Discovery*, May, 1989):

> If the ten billion neurons in the human brain generate electric charges, it might mean that the brain's circuitry is organized along simpler lines than has ever been imagined. Chaos is part of a larger field of mathematics—nonlinear dynamics.

And according to Walter J. Freeman, neurophysiologist at the University of California in Berkeley, that chaotic firing keeps the "millions of nerve cells idling and alive" so that at any time "they can be shifted into gear in response to a stimulus." And we are hearing that chaos is the only type of mechanism that can, without being periodically regular, deal with the uncertain environment of the mind with any kind of control. Stuart Kauffman, a developmental biologist at the University of Pennsylvania School of Medicine, tells us this:

> Organisms might have certain properties not because of selection, but because of the self-organizing properties of those systems on which the selection works. The human genome may be a self-organizing system, it may produce the range

of human cell types on its own, without benefit of
natural selection.

I find this is the appropriate place for an observation
made by Paul Rapp: "The low chaotic buzz of the brain is
the equivalent of an 'I don't know' state."

Many contemporary writers hypothesize that the key to
the origin of life can be found in the original development of
the compounds specific to all living matter. But there are
others who make the statement that the simple laws of ther-
modynamics and kinetics could not have caused the origin of
complex molecules with highly specific functions such as
those of the heart and brain and they see man as part of a
planned creation for life on Earth.

There have been many books written about the physical
man, and by experts. It still does not explain him. This man
that we speak of is neither male nor female, only a life-form
known as *a human*. A human, the most curious of creatures,
is still shrouded in mystery. There is something strangely
unidentifiable and even wonderful about this high form of
animal which we keep tearing apart and putting back together, each time finding something new, something we did-
n't understand before, and we aren't quite sure we do yet.

This animal has deep dark secrets that seem to elude
science. It has talents that as an animal it should not rightly
possess. And it has a mind that moves outside of the world
in which man is supposedly observing all of man, mentally
traveling in places to which the body cannot follow. Our
ESP phenomena (which science today is gradually accepting
as a measurable energy) posits that man's perceptions move
beyond what our sciences consider as the prescribed opera-
tional area of the individual senses of the brain. There is that
part of man that is, and may always be, beyond the compre-
hension of man himself. An unfathomable something that
cannot be seen, felt, tasted, or smelled. But we know intui-

tively that it resides within. This part of man is generally referred to as the soul. This is the part of the human, perhaps the super-human, that religion has been trying to deal with. We hear from the ancient ones that man has not one, but several bodies, each distinct from the material structure of bone and flesh. This belief has been a part of the traditions of Egypt, the Chinese, and the Mayans of Central America. Ancient thinkers speculated as to the precise location of the spiritual faculties of man.

It can easily be said that man, as long as he has been conscious of being conscious, has spent as much energy in search of his soul as he has in uncovering the bases of his physical self. With each new technological advance he digs deeper and deeper into microscopic realms of the human organism, describing and measuring in great detail. Untold volumes of material about this human are available to any of us, with a constant flow of updates, for our study of this Earth life form. Stepping alongside the many biological observations are the great minds of philosophy, posing seemingly unanswerable questions on the union of body and soul. Thomas Aquinas, a thirteenth century theologian and philosopher inquired:

> Does the soul which is somehow compound with
> a body exist as an immaterial substance or prin-
> ciple in such a way as that the being composed of
> body and soul consists of two distinct substances
> or entities...?

David Hume, a Scottish philosopher and historian coming out of the eighteenth century, puts his thought forward as a statement rather than a question. We hear:

> ...there is no principal in all of nature more mys-
> terious than the union of soul and body.

George Berkeley (1685-1753), an Irish bishop and philosopher, chooses to dodge this treacherous, swamp-like area. He claims: "What the soul is and whether it exists be-longs to metaphysics." This very adroitly places the question outside both physiology and philosophy. But Pascal, a French mathematician, physicist, and philosopher is un-daunted and, in poetic fashion philosophizes:

> "What is man? A Nothing in comparison with the Infinite, an all in comparison with the Nothing, a mean between nothing and everything ...he is equally incapable of see-ing the Nothing from which he was made and the Infinite in which he is being swal-lowed up."

It seems that even Jesus was struck by this conception of the real man. Here we have a question attributed to Him as taken from the *Gnostic Gospel* by Elaine Pagels:

> If spirit came into being because of the body, it is a wonder of wonders. Indeed, I am amazed at how this great wealth (the spirit) has made its home in this poverty (the body).

This is the way Gnosticism[1] answers that question:

> Man is composed of flesh, soul and spirit...his origin is two-fold: mundane and extra mundane. Both the body and the soul are products of the cosmic powers who shaped the body in the image of the Primal Man, and animated it with their own physical forces.... Only the innermost or pneumatic man is the true man, and he is not of this world.

The philosophical doctrine of the *Cabala* (*Kabala*: *Kab-bahla*), an ancient interpretation of the scriptures of the Old

---

[1] A system of belief combining ideas derived from Greek philosophy, ori-ental mysticism, and, ultimately, Christianity, stressing salvation through gnosis (intuitive knowledge).

Testament, sees man as being a world within a world within a universe. Within this doctrine we find the belief that man is a microcosm of the universe; a reflection of everything that has ever been or ever will be. These beliefs incorporate the ancient theory that the souls of the entire human race preexisted within a cosmic source, all destined to inhabit material bodies. Each soul, before its entrance into the physical world, consists of male and female united into one being. When the soul descends to this Earth the two genders are separated and animate different bodies. In this philosophy the destiny of the soul is an earthly perfected development of the "germs" (potential) implanted in it, which must ultimately return to the source.

To make this philosophy more easily understood it is depicted as a *Tree of Life* (see diagram opposite Creation section, page 77). This tree consists of ten *sephirot* or realities: crown (Kether: absolute, creative power); wisdom (Hokmah); understanding (Binah); grace (Hesed); power (Geburah); beauty (Tipherath); victory (Netsah); splendour [sic] (Hod); foundation (Yesad); kingdom (Malkuth, physical reality or material world). This, according to the Cabala is the pattern of creation. Man is seen here as a potential god with the *Tree of Life* as his roadmap. In this scheme an advanced soul is seen to be quite capable of working its way back up through these spiritual conceptions to the position of what might be seen on earth as that of a god.

The *Cabala* and Gnosticism see man through similar eyes. But they seem to differ in the harder line which Gnosticism takes toward their gods:

> ...the archons[2] created man for the express purpose of keeping him captive here...incarnation in the outer, material body merely completes the complex imprisonment.

---

[2] Archons: rulers (Webster).

This same thinking comes out of many different philosophies: "Humanity," says Gurdjieff, "like the rest of organic life, exists on Earth for the needs and purpose of the Earth" (*The Gurdjieff Work,* Kathleen Riordan Speeth). And from biologist Alfred Latka we hear:

> All organisms are designed to be collectors and transformers, every species can be looked at as a different type of transformer for capturing and using available energy.

Itzhak Bentov (*Stalking the Wild Pendulum*) sees it this way:

> We living beings play an important role in the evolution of the rudimentary consciousness of our planet.... When we magnify our physical matter very much, we find that we are made mostly of void permeated by oscillating fields...these fields couple as well to the isoelectric field of the planet, which means that the motions of our bodies are transmitted far and wide around the planet.

If man does possess an energy body and it is electromagnetic in nature, it must be possible then to manipulate it artificially. This is the claim of the acupuncturist. We seem to have come a long way from that physical man with all of the recognizable parts: here we are trying to tap in, to identify the non-physical unmeasurable human.

The acupuncture method of relieving pain is based on the belief that the human body is a network of energy lines (not part of the nervous system) and, simply put, these energy lines have "terminals," much like a good transportation system. By stimulating the individual terminals a smooth flowing operation of bioenergy is allowed to circulate through the entire body. Using the railroad analogy, it is as if all the switches are thrown open. The acupoints (chakras), or terminals, respond to any change in flow, acting like resistors in an electrical circuit by adjusting the speed and power of the flow. Can we see this human as an electrical machine? And what images are produced in our minds when we superimpose upon this the following statement from Geoffrey Hodson:

> The decision attributed to the deity to make mankind in his own image introduces a profound and fundamental truth concerning man, namely that in his spiritual, intellectual, psychical and physical nature he is a miniature replica of the whole order of created beings and things.

And, perhaps, we could look at this human as a chemically coordinated computer? This is what P.D. Ouspensky has to say about that:

> The human organism represents a chemical factory planned for the possibility of a very large output. But in the ordinary conditions of life the output of this factory never reaches the full production possible to it, because only a small part of the machinery is used which produces only the quantity of material necessary to maintain its own existence.

Ouspensky (*The Fourth Way*) separates humanity into seven different divisions. The first division he sees as a simplification of all things, a primitive religious orientation, and a linear conception of life.

> A sense of one-dimensional space in relation to the outer world. Everything transpires in a line, as-it were.... In man this is the instinct mind.

The second division of man is explained as being sentimental, involved in emotional religions, having an uncontrolled imagination and acting on the basis of passionate likes and dislikes.

> A sense of two dimensional space. It already
> senses, feels, but it does not think. Everything
> appears to it as genuinely real.

Man in the third form is into theoretical religions. He must
have words and definitions for everything and acts from theory alone.

> A sense of three dimensional space. Logical
> thinking. Philosophical division into *I* and not *I*.
> Positivistic science. Subjection of the personality
> to society and law. Automatism.

1-2-3 (Science): Uses man's present state of consciousness and present functions as an instrument for getting certain results.

4-5-6-7 (Science): Connected with improving the instrument of knowing, with improving man's functions and
state of consciousness.

If I understand Ouspensky correctly he is telling us that
the man of the fifth, sixth, and seventh form is on his way to
becoming one of the gods of our time. This theory dovetails
with the *Cabala* in which man is seen as a potential god.

The theories that have tried to explain man and his place
in his world have come out of, and are still coming through,
all religions, philosophies, and many fields of science. Today's science is still trying to isolate the core or essence of
man. Some researchers feel that somewhere among the test
tubes and plethora of lab equipment they may have cornered
man, but they are still not sure.

Many in these fields of science are trying to deal with
this mysterious life-form outside the implications of creation
and, staying within the confines of the evolutionary theory,
they make the statement that man is a marvelous biological
miracle. Still others claim man is a machine, the human
functions can be measured scientifically, a mechanism along
the premise of a modern radio station, broadcasting vibra-

tions, sending and receiving. They see man as a producer of universal energy. But whatever the theory, we are finding it extremely difficult to place all of man's newly discovered or recognized universal talents within the earth-bound theories of Creation or Evolution.

The fields of medicine, anatomy, and biology have been observing and describing the physical properties of man for thousands of years. More recently, with the invention of electronmicroscopy, the areas of genetics and biomedical engineering have greatly expanded our understanding of the human organism at the cellular level. But we continue to be fascinated by the unknown, the connection between body and soul. We seek out that miraculous wisp—the spirit.

Perhaps the closest we can come to grasping this untouchable, ineffable substance (and what many feel is the most important aspect of the human), is in the area of quantum mechanics and its research into sub-atomic particles.

An article appeared in *Science Digest* (July, 1986) entitled "Reality Anyone" by Gerald Jonas. In this article, the author describes physics experiments where a "single particle can apparently exist in two places at the same time." He goes on to explain that in "delayed choice" research designs, this type of particle appears to take two separate paths simultaneously, but when a "particle detector" is used by the researcher the particle will be found in only one of the two pathways with no indication that it had ever moved along the other path.

The bottom line here is that the research design itself decides the path of the subatomic particles, in effect, "...the experimenter's choice literally determines the shape of reality." He goes on to quote Carroll Alley Jr. (University of Maryland) "The experimental evidence suggests that we have a role in creating the universe."

The hard sciences of physics and chemistry relate that all matter is made up of molecules, their atoms, and of course, individual subatomic particles. Now however, quantum mechanics is hacking away at the Newtonian laws governing physics when subatomic particles are involved. According to Gary Zukav (*The Dancing Wu Li Masters*) subatomic particles do not respond to these orderly behavior patterns and, instead, merely react in terms of probabilities. Specifically, one subatomic particle would have an x% probability of showing up in a certain location, at a certain time and speed, but never could the physicist say exactly what that would be, or even if it would be. Subatomic particles, Zukav explains, merely have "a tendency to happen," the possibility of becoming. Try superimposing this abstract model on the human body—the subatomic particles which are a component of each molecule's atoms in each cell in our body. Imagine these untold trillions of subatomic particles either becoming, or not, perhaps by the conditions we set up out of the simplest of choices we make. If we set up conditions which deny groups of these particles their existence as actual palpable material, do they (or their potential) remain dormant within the body in the form of energy? Or do they bounce around and eventually move through us into some other arena of the cosmos? If this happens, can it happen in large groups of particles and at single instants in time? Would the effect of such a phenomena be the presence or experience of what we describe as "emotion," i.e. depression, anger, and so on? Or could it take its form in more unusual happenings such as telepathy or ESP, or perhaps only that curious sensation most of us report feeling at times, that singular experience of the "me?"

Alan Watts (*The Book*) seemed to parallel this idea when he wrote:

> At the level of existence "I" am immeasurably
> old; my forms are infinite and their comings and
> going are simply the pulses or vibrations of a sin-
> gle and eternal flow of energy.

"Man," says Vera Stanley Alder (*Finding of the Third Eye*) possesses:

> (l)...a solid physical body...of low frequency vibrations through which he contacts physical things.
>
> (2) An etheric body...a body of finer vibrations, acting as a channel through which all the magnetic life-forces are fed to it.
>
> (3) An astral body...having much the same high speed as electricity...
>
> (4) A mental body from which thought travels across the world in a few seconds.
>
> (5) A spiritual body,...composed of the finest and most high frequency vibrations of all.... When man can consciously function in his spirit-body he is able finally to conquer time and space.

And from Louis Pauwels/Jacques Bergier (*The Morning of the Magicians*) we hear:

> The human mind in action uses a most complex machine that it has taken 300,000 years of evolution to perfect; the human body. And the body is never alone, and does not exist alone: it is bound to the Earth and to the whole Cosmos by thousands of material and energy producing links.

So—what is man we ask? What is he besides flesh, blood, and bones and a past dating back perhaps a million years? He has a heart that automates this mass, a brain that directs it. Is it a contrivance of some universal engineer? Or—was he really "created from the dust of the Earth" by some god-like sculptor?

What is Man?

Man, according to Gurdjieff, is evolving from mammal-hood to immortality. "We are still on the mammalian level—robots, controlled by conditioning—sleepwalkers" (*A Study of Gurdjieff's Teaching*, Kenneth Walker).

"Man is an automaton," says P.D. Ouspensky, "depending on outer impulses for his every mood," (*Fourth Dimension*).

"Man, like the cosmos he lives in, is an electromagnetic system," so say Guy Playfair and Scott Hill, "everything he does is guided by E M (electromagnetic) processes" (*The Cycles of Heaven*).

Immortality is possible according to Paul Segall, Ph.D., researcher at U.C. Berkeley. "We are not the chemicals," he says, "man is the pattern—the mathematical blueprint—a formula for immortality. DNA is the programming system—cybernetics is the key."

This question has intrigued philosophers, poets, and scientists. The theologians chopped away at relegating their one explanation to a world of obscure fantasy. Geologists used picks and shovels while scientists stayed with their test tubes, their calculating machines, and physical anthropologists ran alongside, measuring the distance between man and his closest relative—the ape.

Out of all of this the explanations that are being given as an answer to this persisting question range from pre-Darwinian beliefs to a variety of vacillating scenarios on "Man is an animal." So—again we pursue the question "What or Who is Man?"

Who am I? I am Man

I was born of the sea and grew in the forests, the dark caves once were home and fire was my first miracle. I moved with the hunted and the hunter and brushed lives with the giants of a world that was lost in baptisms of fire, wind, and water. Rising from a sanctuary of mud I walked within the shadows of "gods" who did instill within me "soul," a softly nagging neighbor to whom I am considerably indebted and by whom I am constantly coerced. Within me fear walks side by side with arrogance, and the mind that did come to me through the hands of those gods is that which is called consciousness and is that part of "seeing" which comes without the slightest movement of an eye. But I am alone, and I must act accordingly, placing one foot in front of the other, and each step must be of my own making. At the same time I am a small part of a "whole" and I must take into consideration those other singular parts of the whole that follow the same path. I am one. I am all, I am man.

Am I the invention of a Great Creator cradled in the womb of a human? If I am only a whim of nature what do I claim as my birthright? God claims me, man seeds me, nature nurses me, and Heaven binds me. To whom, or what, do I owe homage?

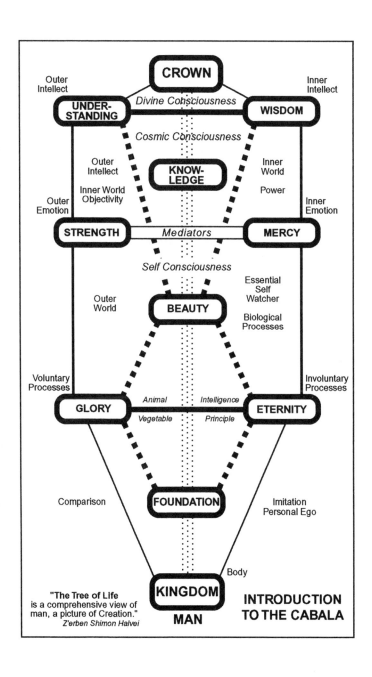

CROWN

Outer Intellect

Inner Intellect

UNDER-STANDING

Divine Consciousness

WISDOM

Cosmic Consciousness

Outer Intellect

KNOW-LEDGE

Inner World

Inner World Objectivity

Power

Outer Emotion

Inner Emotion

STRENGTH

Mediators

MERCY

Self Consciousness

Essential Self Watcher

Outer World

BEAUTY

Biological Processes

Voluntary Processes

Involuntary Processes

GLORY

Animal *Intelligence*

ETERNITY

Vegetable *Principle*

Comparison

FOUNDATION

Imitation Personal Ego

Body

KINGDOM

MAN

"The Tree of Life is a comprehensive view of man, a picture of Creation."
Z'erben Shimon Halvei

INTRODUCTION TO THE CABALA

CREATION

> In the beginning God created the heaven and the
> earth. And the earth was without form, and void;
> and darkness was upon the face of the deep. Day
> and night were created on the first day; The sky
> and ocean were formed on the Second day. Dry
> land emerged and plants and trees "burst forth"
> from the earth on the third day. On the fourth
> day, the sun and moon were brought into being.
> The birds, fish, and sea creatures were created on
> the fifth day, with wild animals, cattle, and rep-
> tiles following on the sixth day. And on that same
> sixth day...God said, let us make man in our im-
> age....(Genesis, *Holy Bible,* King James Version)

For me the question is, did life originate on Earth or did
it originate somewhere else in the galaxy? We have many-
theories.

From the readings of Edgar Cayce we have:

> In the beginning was the spirit, occupying all
> space, all time.... Amelius the first creation by
> necessity was endowed with free will and reason,
> otherwise he would remain of the whole, at the
> will of the whole.

Taken from *The Hidden Wisdom of the Holy Bible Vol.II*
by Geoffrey Hodson, we have the Hebrew words *iaphah*
(meaning, he breathed), *aphio* (meaning, inspired—the inspirational faculty of living soul), *Nishemath* (meaning, to
elevate, to enoble, being raised to a higher state, becoming
an individual human soul).

The English translation is, according to Hodson, "He
breathed into his nostrils the breath of life and man became a
living soul."

The Interpreter's Bible contains two accounts of the
creation of the world by God. According to the first (Genesis

l:2-25), man was created male and female (asexual form). If we follow the second version (Genesis 24:13-25), man was created first, then the trees, the animals and finally, woman.

The Hebrew *Pentateuch* places the Creation or Era (Anno Mundi) at 4004 B.C. The *Septuagint* places the Creation at 5872 B.C. The Talmudists' *Pentateuch* places the Creation at 5344 B.C., and the Josephus at 4658 B.C.

From Egypt's *Book of the Dead:*[3]

> I, the evolver of the evolutions, evolved myself, the evolver of all evolutions; after many evolutions and developments, which come forth from my mouth. No heaven existed and no earth and no terrestrial animals or reptiles had come to be. I formed them out of an inert mass of watery matter...none other worked with me. I laid the foundation of all things by my will, and all things evolved themselves therefrom. I united myself to my shadow and set forth Shu and Tefnut out of myself; thus being one God. I contained three and Shu and Tefnut gave birth to Nut and Set and Nut gave birth to Osiris, Horus—Khens—Ana—Maa, Sut, Isis, and Netheys, at one birth. One right after the other, and their children multiply upon the earth.

Recorded evidence suggests the Egyptians had a specific belief about the way that man was created. A bas-relief commemorating the birth of Amenhotep III (1411-1375 BC) at Luxor shows the ram-headed fertility god, Khnum, fash-

---

[3] Egyptian *Book of the Dead*: a collection of ancient religious writings dating back to the 16th century B.C. It deals with the spiritual dangers of the other world: judgement, resurrection, and immortality.

ioning the infant king and his ka (other self) on a potter's wheel.

From *The Mayan Book of the Dawn* translation by Dennis Tedlock we have this:

> The First Four Humans, the first four earthly be-
> ings who were truly articulate when they moved
> their feet and hands, their face and mouths, and
> who could speak the very language of the gods,
> could also see everything under the sky and on
> the earth....But then the gods, who had not in-
> tended to make the model beings with the poten-
> tial of becoming their own equals, limited human
> sight to what was obvious and nearby....

The Mayan Book of the Dawn is to the Mayans what the Bible is to western religions. Sometimes the variations within both of these are relegated to the realm of myth. But we are beginning to believe that all myths come out of a dimly remembered bit of past history. The similarities seem to indicate different perspectives of observing and recording the same experience, the same event. The Mayans make the claim that a god, Heart-of-the-Earth-and-Sky made creatures out of clay to rule the world but destroyed them each time until one model satisfied this Creator and was allowed to live. This story of creation is almost identical to the one of Adam and Eve, even to the creating gods becoming fearful of their creation because this new life-form showed promise of "becoming like god's son."

The idea of an original creation by a single all-powerful Creator comes to the western world through the Hebrew prophet Moses. It was Moses who made known the para-doxical, mysterious nature of this Creator. Brahma, in many writings, has been credited with creating the Earth, but the followers of the Buddhist scriptures boastfully declare their freedom from any personal belief in a Creator. Following the "silence of the Buddha," they show no interest in the questions of creator or the infinity and eternity of this world and its universe. "It matters not whether the beginning of things is revealed." But we also hear this (speaking of Swayamb-huva, the Lord who exists through himself):

> Having been impelled to produce various beings from his own divine substance, he first mani-fested the waters which developed within them-selves a production seed, the seed became a germ bright as gold, blazing like a luminary with a thousand beams, and in that egg he was born himself, in the form of Brahma, the great princi-ple of all beings (Manu, Book I, Slokas 8, 9).

The Cabala (Kabala) speaks about "the endless emana-tions of the one First Cause," all of which became gradually transformed by popular perception into gods, spirits, angels, and demons who became almost human and were given names and generally assigned a limited existence. In the Nazarene[4] or Bordesanian System, which is often thought of as the Kabala within the Kabala, Fetahil is considered the architect of the visible universe. This is the story that came out of Daniel J. Boorstin's *The Creators*:

> Abatur opens a gate and walks to the dark water (Chaos), and looking down into it, the darkness reflects the image of Himself, and lo! a son is formed—the Logos or Demiurge; Fetahil who is the builder of the material world. In this way the substance of the universe is brought into exis-tence. According to Gnostic dogma, this was Metatron, the Archangel Gabriel, or messenger of life.

The creation stories that come to us from all corners of our world have similar allegorical interpretations, unusual only in the use of unfamiliar names and perspective coming

---

[4] Christian of Jewish origin.

out of strange, to us, societies. From the philosophy of China comes the belief that "in the beginning there was Yin and Yang." But:

> Before the beginning of days—before the earth was formed or the sky there was Tao, the Great Original Cause. All things came from Tao and on Tao all depend.

And then "P'an Ku came forth" and began arranging the Yin and Yang in many forms.

The simplicity of some of these myths coming out of our world's less well known cultures fit nicely into children's literature. Here are a few taken from the writings of Sophia L. Fahs and Dorothy T. Spoerl (*Beginnings: Earth, Sky, Life, and Death*):

> Olelbis, The-Great-One-Who-Sits-Above-the-Sky in the Beautiful Land of Olelpanti, is the god of the Wintu Indians who once lived at the northern tip of California. Olelbis, The Great-One-Who-Sits-Above-the-Sky, was lonely so he created a new race of men. But they tell us that before there were any Indians living, there was another very different race of men on earth and as the earth became crowded they began to fight each other. Then Olelbis turned those people into other kinds of living creatures to live alongside the new race of men and he wanted them to live happily and peacefully together. But he was not sure how he could make this happen. So he asked himself, 'What shall I do? How can I help them?' Then he thought 'Perhaps if I make them immortal, maybe then they will be happy. I will have them live forever. They shall never die.' But Sedit, the old Coyote man, cried out, 'No! That is not good. Let man die.' And the animals all agreed. And came to the conclusion that man must die if he is to experience the gladness of

birth and the sorrow of death and through these
two things together man comes to know love.

African bushmen tell of a god who, long, long ago, ruled
in a land where people never died. Bushmen of the Kalahari
Desert tell stories of their god Kaang, the Great Master and
Lord of All Life, whose world was under the earth where the
people were never hungry or sick and they never died. But
Kaang became restless, he dreamed of the wonders he could
create in the world above. So Kaang made a marvelous tree
grow out of the earth, the roots reached down into the secret
underground world where the people were living. Near the
roots Kaang dug a hole and when the hole was finished
Kaang called the first-of-all-men to climb to the top of the
earth. When the last of the people and animals had come up
to the surface of the earth Kaang disappeared, hiding himself
somewhere up in the sky where he could watch over them.

In a story coming from the Zuni Indians of New Mexico,
the Sun-Father is seen as the creator of the Four-Fold-
Containing-Earth-Mother. And we are told three of these
"Folds" were dark caves under the earth and the fourth was
the land that we know today. Here is part of the story from
Beginnings: Earth, Sky, Life and Death by Sophia L. Fahs
and Dorothy T. Spoerl:

> In the far-off beginning, there was no earth or
> sky. Only a watery waste with the Sun-Father
> above. There were no animals; and no people.
> For ages uncounted the Sun-Father shone on the
> watery waste until, because of the warmth of his
> great light, a green scum began to grow on top of
> the great waters. Slowly the scum spread. It grew
> wider and wider and thicker and thicker until at
> last it became the Four-Fold-Containing-Earth-
> Mother.

> The deepest level was a dark, damp cave called the Cave of the Sooty Depth. Here were the seeds of men.

And after many ages the seeds grew into living things that crawled like reptiles, not caring where they went or what they did. Then the Sun-Father shone upon the waters and out of the foam that floated upon the waters arose two beautiful gods, Beloved Twaine. Then Beloved Twaine went down into the Cave of the Sooty Depth and weaving a ladder from vines brought man up, directing his evolution cave by cave until he rose to the level of the Four-Fold-Containing-Earth Mother, the world of the upper air which we know. Because of Beloved Twaine man grew.

This story of the beginning was told by the Norsemen. It is from a very old collection of poems, the Elder Edda, stories told by grandmothers, about the beginning of man (*Worlds in Collision,* Immanuel Velikovsky); this tale of creation also speaks of disorder and darkness.

> When time began, all was chaos—that is, nothing was formed or in order. There was neither sea nor sand nor salty wave. There was neither earth nor sky.
>
> In the center of space was a wide, dark, and deep cavern called Gin-nung-ga-gap. On one side of this dark cavern was the place of cold and darkness called Niffl-heim. Huge icebergs, covered with cold mist and frost, rose like mountains. On the other side of the cavern was the place of warmth and light, called Mus-pell-heim. There mountains of fire sent their sparks upward and across the deep dark cavern.
>
> And the sparks from the flaming mountains of Mus-pell-heim, fell on the icy blocks of Gin-nung-ga-gap and caused all the blocks of ice to become coated with layers of salty frost. And out

of that salty frost arose Yemir, the frost giant on the first day; and on the third day there rose Buri, the first of the Good Gods to live on the earth. Buri in time had three grandsons, Odin, Vile, and Ve who slew Yemir the frost giant and from Yemir's skull built the dome of the sky. Then these same three Good Gods caught the red-hot sparks from the flaming mountains and threw them up into the sky where the largest became the moon and the others stars. Many ages passed and the earth became beautiful, but no human had been born. The three Good Gods took it upon themselves to correct this by carving Man from a fallen ash tree and woman from a fallen elm. They called man Ask and the woman Embla, and from these two first humans all others descended. So the story goes in essence.

In a story of creation coming out of Babylon we again meet with the names Marduk and Tiamat that we encountered in the creation of Earth. Unlike the story of Marduk the Twelfth Planet, destructively meeting the old planet Tiamat, we have, in this telling, Marduk the mighty grandson destroying his grandmother, Tiamat, purely for political reasons (*Gods, Graves and Scholars,* C.N. Ceram).

For hundreds of years, during the New Year's Festival, the high priest of Babylon chanted this poem of creation and it is assumed that parts of it were dramatized for the benefit of an audience. But the story is Sumerian and was taken from seven clay tablets excavated at the site of the famous ancient city of Nineveh and translated into English by Dr. E.A. Speiser of the University of Pennsylvania. The shortened version found in the work of Sophia Lyon Fahs and Dorothy T. Spoerl, has been in this telling reduced to a carefully compiled synopsis which begins like this:

When above no heaven had been created, And below no earth had yet appeared, Nothing had

> been separated from anything else. Apsu, the
> spirit of fresh water, and Tiamat, the spirit of salt
> water, moved quietly within the watery deep,
> Apsu and Tiamat, the First Father and First
> Mother of all that is.

After "unmeasured time" passed other gods were born, both sexes, and they had children who produced grandchildren. Now they were all wiser and stronger and taller than Apsu and Tiamat but not as peaceful. Their loud laughter and constant activity disturbed Apsu, and although Tiamat "loathed" their behavior she refused to reprimand them. Apsu suggested to Tiamat that they destroy the children so that they might have, again, peace and quiet. Tiamat became angry at the suggestion that they should kill all those lives that they had created. But Apsu's counselor quietly urged the First Father to secretly destroy the children. Tiamat need not know. But the secret found its way among the gods and they decided that Apsu had gone too far this time.

The rebellious ones growled and raged while preparing for battle although Ea was the only one bold enough to confront his grandfather. Ea brewed a magic spell that put First Father into a deep sleep. With Apsu in this state Ea tore the jewels from the wrist and the crown from the head of Apsu and placed it upon his own, declaring himself king.

Tiamat must have revenge. The Great Mother created many monsters to go into battle with her. Ea went forth to fight Tiamat but at the sight of her he turned back faint-hearted.[5] Ea's son, Marduk, volunteers to take his father's place and went forth to slay the terrible Tiamat. Tiamat and her monsters fought savagely but Marduk enfolded her in a

---

[5] An illustration (p. 67 *Beginnings)* depicts Tiamat as part bird and part beast. The lower half shows a Winged, feathered body with bird tail and feet. The upper half are the head and front paws of what looks to be an angry jaguar.

86

magic net and then pierced her heart with an arrow. When Tiamat died the monsters fell back into an inanimate state. Marduk split the body of Tiamat into two parts, half became the sky and from the lower half earth was created.

The author believes that all the myths wound around that beginning—the creation of man and his world, belong to a universal history. And that history has been kept alive through the accepted medium of mythology. There are few narratives in any system, religious or otherwise, that do not have at their center some historical foundation. But in the ancient world of myth and legend we have gods climbing up from the bowels of the Earth and dropping down from the sky. Today we see our world as an Empire of Galaxies. Earth a small star and our gods are Intelligent Beings from Space. Our Biblical characters in the Garden of Eden move out of a Sumerian history, posturing space-men as the progenitors of life on Earth. The originator of Adam. The AUTHOR of Man.

Man's new sciences make it possible to reach into the depths of space. To probe, to find many planets in our heaven, some like Earth, may be capable of evolving and supporting life. With new "eyes" astronomers track the speeding heavenly bodies always moving away from man and his small world. On the ground archeologists search for man by examining the stone tools and artifacts he has left behind; anthropologists seek out the sites of ancient societies, seeing them as the "beginning" of our modern human. And geologists are cataloguing the changes in our Earth's formation and environment which tell a story covering millions of years.

Man's ancient unknowable history, animal behaviorists believe, can be traced through the learning abilities and genetic structure of monkeys as measured against similarities in modern man. Psychologists probe the human brain while paleoanthropologists look at man's potential development through an ancient world of fossils. And in this way western man destroys his own Creation story and builds in its place a theory of evolution.

On the edge of the forest, a strange, old fashioned animal still hesitated. His body was the body of a tree dweller, and, though tough and knotty by human standards, he was, in terms of that world into which he gazed, a weakling. His teeth, though strong for chewing on the tough fruits of the forest or for crunching an occasional unwary bird caught with his prehensile hands, were not the tearing sabers of the great cats. He had a passion for lifting himself up to see about, in his restless, roving curiosity. He would run, a little stiffly and uncertainly perhaps, on his hind legs, but only in those rare moments when he ventured out upon the ground. All this was the legacy of his climbing days: he had a hand with flexible fingers and no fine hoofs upon which to gallop like the wind.

He was a ne'er-do-well, an in-betweener. Nature had not done well by him. It was as if she had hesitated and never quite made up her mind. Perhaps as a consequence, he had a malicious gleam in his eye, the gleam of an outcast who has been left nothing and knows he is going to have to take what he gets. One day, a little band of these odd apes—for apes they were—shambled out upon the grass: the human story had begun.

Loren Eiseley, *The Star Thrower*

EVOLUTION

> **Evolution**, n. 1. evolushun; 2. ...P.P. type of evolvere, to unroll, unfold....l. an unrolling, unfolding, esp. by a gradual and natural process of gradual development wherever exhibited; esp. the evolution of a drama, the gradual unfolding of the plot as expressed in the action. 2. (bill.) The course of development by natural processes, as seen in the animated world of nature, whether it affects the growth of the individual organism or that of the species; the doctrine of evolution is opposed to the creationist view; the latter holds that each variety in vegetable and animal kingdoms was produced by a special creative act, whereas the doctrine of evolution is that all the innumerable varieties, species and genera were gradually developed, or evolved, from few simple ancestral forms or types. (Webster's Dictionary).

> "...geological evolution is seen as the result of processes of mountain-building, sedimentation, and erosion that have gone on throughout the history of the earth, at least since the time when liquid water was present in appreciable quantities." A.N. Whitehead, (*Science and the Modern World*).

Evolution, as it was first grasped scientifically, was enthusiastically seen as a smooth moving assembly-line operation. A generalized moving-picture of man from the "beginning" to the present. The beginning being a primeval "soup" in which simple molecules crowded together to form an invisible bit of life, which quite possibly, lost out to Mother Nature many times before conditions were such that it was allowed to live and multiply. That small primary cell, with the assistance of a gratifying fortuitous spark, is hypothesized as being responsible for all of the various life forms in the world today.

Edward Edelson (*Who Goes There: The Search for Intelligent Life in the Universe*) sees lightning as a trigger for the sudden life-giving movement of inert energies, and nickel clay as the catalyst. He explains that many clays destroy a large number of amino acids while zinc uniquely concentrates the nucleotides that make up DNA, the formula for life on Earth.

> ...it is quite possible for a single molecule and its descendants to be responsible for all life on Earth today. And, it is also quite possible for the formation of cells to be accidental, depending entirely on coincidence.

Doctor Cyril Ponnamperuma, Director of the Laboratory of Chemical Evolution at the University of Maryland, claims to have proven that all five bases that are necessary for the life-giving DNA and RNA can be made in "one fell swoop" when electric sparks are passed through an atmosphere of methane, nitrogen, and water.

> The doctrine of evolution undertakes to explain the origin and development of the various forms of plant and animal life on earth, both past and present. This doctrine has its foundation in certain unities in nature which are universally existent and demonstrable. Chief among these are; the unity of action of the process of nature; the unity of structure in plants and animals; the unity in the mode of reproduction; the presence of protoplasm as the material base for all life. (*The Encyclopedia of Philosophy, Vol.I*)

Natural selection is the name of all processes whereby some genotypes developed an advantage over others. Natural selection seems to be the most reasonable explanation for the distribution of genes observed in human populations. Evolution occurs when new genetic traits appear in a population by means of mutation. But the individual life form in which the mutation appears must have a reproductive advantage: the survival of the fittest.

The story of evolution might easily be pictured as bits of greenery floating on a watery surface; thriving, gathering soil and forming small islands where tiny life forms would make their debut. At first they are hardly noticeable, but then in a moment of Earth-time they can be observed by the naked eye. A tropical panorama of birth.

To say that this theoretical paradise could be a Garden of Eden might be speculatively in keeping with the picture. But logically, in this green Earthy community, we should expect to find one leafy and lofty growth battling its neighboring foliage for acquisition of the soil on those islands. And a tiny bit of algae might suddenly decide it has helped in the creation of a monster as it stares helplessly into the hungry open mouth of a fish. The competitive spirit must have been there at the beginning, an instinctive contest of survival in Mother Nature's nursery.

Evolution is a process within which a simple form of life grows into a more complex form through periodic changes known as mutations. Bacteria are believed to be the simplest and the first living organisms and there are tens of thousands of different bacteria species. Now it is being discovered that these simplest of life-forms can measure and monitor their environment, making judgements about the conditions of their life: "...they are, in fact, remarkably complicated enigmas." So says Howard Berg, Biologist (*Smithsonian*, Sept., 1983). And he has found, in his experiments with these smallest of creatures, that they can, if they don't agree with what is happening around them, do something about it.

It's hard to imagine the millions of years and billions of mutations that must have come in between the enigmatic bacteria and the first appearance of the invertebrate six hundred million years ago. And four hundred million years ago, according to Robert Jastro (*Until the Sun Dies*), "the fishes left the sea and built an alien world along the shores."

> ...the first vertebrate to appear, (John Pfieffer, *The Emergence of Man*) from what ancestor nobody knows, was the jawless astracodern. They flourished for millions of years in a wide variety of forms which suggests that the class was already old when the most ancient fossils were forming.

The lack of fossil evidence led us to believe that there had been no evolutionary activity prior to six hundred million years ago. But there are several theories that might explain the missing precambrian fossils: one has to do with the destruction of the fossil record by intense heat and pressure, perhaps a close encounter with a runaway comet? Another sees this as a time for movement of primitive life from bodies of water to land. Still another has to do with the supposed lack of oxygen present in our atmosphere at that time. In spite of that, however, evidence from the Earth's crust tells us that bacteria and bluegreen algae were present in our world as early as thirty one hundred million years ago.

There may have been several mass extinctions since the appearance of the invertebrates; men of science believe that about two hundred and twenty-five million years ago a good half of the species of organisms died out on the planet in a comparatively short span of time. Would the break up of a super land mass, the time estimated as approximately two hundred million years ago, have something to do with this? At that time a large continent, now described by some as Pangea, broke into two continents—Laurasia in the north and Gondwanaland in the south. About sixty-five to seventy million years ago, Africa was moving in on Europe, Australia became separated from Antarctica, and India was becoming a part of Asia.

We are now being told that the continents reached their present geographical positions about seventy million years ago. And, according to the information passed on to us by science, in this same period Earth's largest terrestrial animal, the dinosaur, died out and man entered the scene. Now we would like to ask: did the movement of land have something to do with the extinction of one class of animal—the dinosaur, and the appearance of another—man?

The human's present traceable evolutionary story seems to emerge along a very crooked thoroughfare, moving into a modern conception of a beginning through the findings of archeological excavations. A story told by bones and teeth. The difference between man and monkey measured in the size of a cranium and an upright body on straight legs.

From excavated bone fossils we are learning that the evolution from ape to Homidae and the vertical position seemed to enter our world in spasmodic leaps rather than the theorized slow moving methodical forward march. It reads something like this: Three million years ago an ape-man with a heavy built skull and very big cheek teeth occupied one branch of the Hominid family tree. He came to be known as Australopithecus robustus ("the robust southern ape"). Quietly homesteading another branch of the same tree was an ape-man with a more lightly fashioned cranium and smaller teeth, named Australopithecus africanus ("the southern ape of Africa"). In South Africa, especially since the twenties, archeological excavations have brought to light a large number of fossil ape skeletons which would seem to be part of a very large family, the Australopithecines (*austra-*

lius/south, *pithecus*/apes). The australo-pithecines had an average brain capacity of less than 600 c.c.[1]

The Australopithecines, dating back a million years, were apes with the exception of larger brain capacity and the hip and thigh (femur), leg (tibia/fibula), and foot bones are definitely man-like. Fossils have been found in many parts of the Old World—Europe, Africa, India, China—but it always appears that Robustus and Africanus were moving side by side without any recognizable signs of having evolved one from the other. But to get on with the story, going back two million years we might find Australopithecus Africanus traveling under the name of Homo habilis ("man the handy man"). And, apparently he had a companion. Science claims there were at least two proto human species at that time. I am not sure Robustus was part of that scene. But, logically, either one of them could have been the root stock of Homo erectus *this man who walks upright.*

Homo erectus was distinguished mainly by a large cranial cavity with a mean value of more than 1100 c.c., but with a range variation from around 900 c.c. to almost 2000 c.c., surpassing Homo sapiens' ("the wise man") 1350 c.c. to 1600 c.c. Five hundred thousand years ago, some of our ancestors had become separated from Homo erectus to a point of specific classification as Homo sapiens. One hundred thousand years ago, Homo sapiens could be found in three different parts of the world.

It might sound simple. Like we are dealing with one genus or specie at a time. But actually out of the family Homidae we have genus Rampithecus—which we have heard of—and Bramapithecus—which up to now has been a stranger. And then we have the species which include R.punjibilicus, R.brevirostris, and Brampithecus thorpee. The Homo genus starts with the Australopithecines and fol-

---

[1]Cubic centimeter, a unit of measure equal to 1/100 meter (.3937 inch).

lows through with fifteen different types, names given these skeletal finds by their discovers. The genus is then divided up into species which are categories of similarity. But I do believe that we are confused enough by now, and if there is a reader who has the fortitude to follow this to the bitter end I would suggest a text, *The Origins of Man*, author John Buettner-Janusch, Duke University.

The Neanderthals followed in the Footsteps of Homo sapiens, a skull unearthed in the Neander river valley (tal/thal/valley) introduced us to this new ancestor. The Neanderthals had an extended range from western Europe to parts of Russia and Central Asia. The earliest date from 130,000 years ago, but most Neanderthals postdate 74,000 years. The last of the Neanderthals died around 32,000 years ago. The Neanderthal man lacked a chin, but the body skeleton was fully adapted to upright movement, and he had a cranial capacity of about 1550 c.c; larger than that of contemporary man. It is believed that Neanderthal man was never exterminated, merely absorbed into another group of homidae. This is where Cro-magnon man came on the scene. And this may be where we lost Neanderthal man.

An abrupt change came about 35,000 years ago. An evolutionary leap. And I understand that if there was any single time that could be claimed as the moment our evolving man became a human, it was at this time, 35,000 years ago.

Cro-Magnon man who made his appearance at that time was tall, handsome, smooth skinned; looking very much like a modern man and with a brain size of 1660 c.c. The Cro-magnon are most admired for art which can be found in those caves in France that were occupied by them; like the rock paintings at Lascaux. And they seemed to have brought with them the ability to create musical instruments and fired-clay sculpture; accordingly there is the belief that Cro-magnon man did not evolve on Earth; rather, he was an invader. And there is the thought that the Cro-magnon invasion could have been death for the Neanderthal. But a puzzling new culture seemed to spring up about then that coexisted alongside the Cro-magnon, the Chatelperronians.[2] It is believed that this was Neanderthal's way of surviving.

The notion that contemporary Homo sapiens, the many races into which it is divided developed from distinct species of Pleistocene Homidae, is not today being supported by any fossil record. Within the facts of man's Earth history the traceable descent of man gives one the feeling of having met with all the dead-end snares of a cleverly engineered maze, without an inkling of which turn might lead to the much desired exit.

Charles Darwin was not the first to consider the process of evolution as a possible answer to that nagging question as to the beginning of man. Hundreds of years before the birth of Christ, philosophers were rationalizing that man, if one were to think logically, must have risen out of some simpler form of life. Aristotle not only believed that animals evolved from animals, but he also theorized that animals rose up out of lifeless matter. Life could evolve from any lifeless matter providing that it was helped along by the elements of air, fire, and water. This combination he called soul.

Saint Augustine (4th century) speaks of the creation of things by a series of causal factors. Leibnitz, two hundred years before Darwin, believed in the universal connection between species with changes brought on by environment. LaMarck (born 1744 and considered the true father of the modern evolution theory) believed that all organisms developed from simple one-cell life forms and were gradually modified by the inherited results of environmental influences to more complex forms.

---

[2] Jared Diamond, "The-Great Leap Forward," *Discover,* May 1989.

Many eminent thinkers of the seventeenth and eighteenth centuries accepted the theory of spontaneous life or generation. Writers tried to verbally persuade the public that there was proof that spontaneous life was not only possible but was actually the way all life had begun. Then in 1860 Louis Pasteur proved, by experimentation, that there was no such thing as spontaneous generation. Life could not spontaneously emerge. Mice were not birthed by a combination of moist soil and sun. Within the heated battle of pros and cons that flared up between the evolutionists there rose the strident voice of the creationists who were bound to damn both sides of the argument as blasphemy. The noisy debate that grew out of man's theories on the beginning of man found Erasmus Darwin, grand-father of Charles, a loud voice on the side of evolution.

Charles Darwin had no use for the term evolution. His feeling was that it did not do justice to his hypothesis of "descent with modification." Darwin, I believe, should be regarded as the correlator of all material on the beginning of man through natural evolution presented up to that time.

Basing his theory on the work of others, he then sought out physical evidence as a foundation on which to build his extended works. Darwin had the courage to put his largely unpopular theory into book form, *The Origin of The Species,* and place it in front of a hostile, creation-minded public. While theology was busily trying to widen the gap between animal and man, Darwin was speaking of, as an evolutionary ancestor of man, a close animal ancestor who possessed the knowledge to build tools from sticks and rocks. Darwin made it possible to deal with the beginning of man outside the doctrine of creation. He was the speaker for that era; an era of social and economic change. Man, at that time, was the seeker of a new god; science was the new god he would choose to follow, and Darwin was its leader. A new religion was being formed. The religion of scientific evolution and its role as a process within which, quite possibly, lay a scientifically provable beginning for man.

Darwin never did find his "missing link." That smooth-moving, knowledge-consuming, intellectually aspiring, evolving brainchild should have left some footprint. Or *mindprint* as Thoreau would probably have termed it. Glen G. Strickland (*Genesis Revisited*), says the following:

> There are not just a few missing links, whole sections of the chain are missing. Millions of life-forms have, supposedly, slid off that constantly moving, man-creating assembly line. But—when we go back more than a couple million years, the relics showing the evolution of our species are rather doubtful.

Darwin himself became very uncertain about his own beliefs; he found that many pieces of the puzzle did not fit the complicated theory of man being the end result of an automatic gesture on the part of Mother Nature. Here we have him asking:

> How can anything so intricate and complex as the human eye have evolved. To suppose the eye with all its inimitable contrivances for adjusting the focus to different distances, for admitting different amounts of light, and for the correction of spherical and chromatic aberrations, could have been formed by natural selection seems, I freely confess, absurd to the-highest degree.[3]

There are many things about man, it seems, that do not fit easily into the picture of natural evolution. Too many to analyze individually and in detail. Too many to allow us to blindly accept natural selection as man's ancestral heritage.

The questionable in-betweens leave too much to the imagination to be accepted as sound, logical theory when

---

[3] Stephen Jay Gould, *Ever Since Darwin.*

dealing with the evolution of advanced life. This is the way that professor Wilder-Smith (*Herfunft Und Zukunft des Menchen*) explains it.

> The intermediate stages arising in the course of evolution cannot fulfill any purpose, as they are completely useless. As an example I may quote the complicated structure which the female whale possesses in order to suckle her young under water without drowning. One cannot imagine any intermediate stage on the way from a normal nipple to a completely developed whale nipple which is suitable for underwater suckling. It was either complete and ready to function or it was not. If it is claimed that such a system develop gradually by chance mutation, that means condemning all whale babies to a watery grave during an evolutionary period lasting thousands of years. To deny planning in the elaboration of such a system strains our credulity more than the invitation to believe in an intelligent nipple constructor, who incidentally, must have had a very sound knowledge of hydraulics.

Evolution, to be scientifically acceptable, must be able to explain step by step, without any element of surprise, the emergence of a species in separate individual changes (mutations). In that way only then will evolution become a true science. As it is now we have only a frustrating theory which comes together like a giant jigsaw puzzle that has many of its pieces missing.

Many scientific minds, searching through bones and time for the human that cannot be seen, realistically, as part of a mythical creation, are haunted by that ape-man who keeps disappearing and then popping back up unexpectedly, sometimes introducing significant and unexplainable changes. Now man is asking the very same questions he was asking before his science adopted the theory of evolution as the unfolder of scientific facts holding all the answers. Now this man is looking more closely at himself and his closest kin and asking, "did man actually descend from a member of the monkey family?" Or, since there is no solid link between ape and man in a positive, evolutionary way, was ape a descendent of man? Something left over from a destroyed, highly civilized man-age? Possible? P.D. Ouspensky (*Tertium Organum*) gives us this:

> ...if we consider the existing forms on any given plane, it will be quite impossible to declare that all these evolved from the simplest forms on this plane. Some undoubtedly evolved from the lowest ones; a third class developed from the remnants of some evolved form... while a fourth class resulted as a consequence of the incursion into the given plane of the properties and characteristics of some higher plane....

Maybe man was not progressing as seen in the imaginary picture of evolution; man was, quite possibly, regressing. Perhaps man's civilization did not begin with the discovery of the wheel; it could be that man had regressed through some cataclysmic event to a point where he had to find a way to move upon the ground because he had forgotten how—or was no longer capable of rising above it. There is no evidence that could deny this. Neither is there evidence that could point, factually, to man's rising emotionally, intelligently, and physically out of the energy of an infinitesimal single cell. There are many unexplained instances that seem to deny that this was the unquestionable one and only door through which man could have made his entrance into his world.

There is a high point of persuasion in the summation of our present-day evolutionary "facts." A type of logic, which we claim, makes these so called "facts" the actual history of mankind without any need to allow another perspective to enter into the making of man's Earth history. If evolution, as we see it now, were to be considered a verifiable "truth," we would then be in the position of having to embrace that which, to a logical mind, seems highly improbable: the theory that man and his world were brought into existence, designed by a thing called "luck." Maybe coincidence or chance, but something that can be seen only as a gamble against long odds. The meeting of spark and cell. The right place. The right time.

Darwin would, no doubt, be delighted with the present day progress of evolutionary biology. He might be overwhelmed by the assemblage of fossil hominids dating back millions of years that are now a part of man's evolutionary history that was set in motion by his statement that "man has evolved wholly by natural means." He believed that man was the end product of a long line of "modified" life forms. "Endless forms most beautiful and most wonderful."

A good part of our world's population said he was right. But those who believed that man could only be the noble work of a god-like sculptor took it upon themselves to defend their belief with words from the Bible which were established in a faith that, according to those of that faith, needed no proof. But, they still demanded proof of any other. And they declared they were right. Whole books, and many, have been written about both convictions without answering even one of the questions that continues to pursue mankind.

Darwin's hypothesized moving picture of man's evolution has been forwarded by today's men of science and now reads something like this: a single cell was the beginning of it all—growing—surviving many changes as land replaced water. This species developed lungs, acquired feet where once there had been fins, and took off over land in search of food. The final pre-human animal was a furry body loping around on all fours at first, then standing unsteadily, and finally moving more solidly on two hind legs. Just one of our biped ancestors, they say.

To move this along according to archaeology, our biped ancestors evolved eventually into family type cave dwellers and were climbing the ladder toward a high civilization. But here is where our slow-moving, constantly evolving ancestors lose their part in this picture, for they must have been around when "all evil was loosed from the Heavens," and the world was lost to fire and water.

Here is a description of an archaeological dig that actually found evidence of a huge flood. This was taken from Werner Keller's *The Bible and History*:

> The next baskets that came to the surface gave an answer that none of the expedition would have dreamed of.... Under the clay deposit almost ten feet thick they had struck fresh evidence of human habitation. Above the mud strata were jars and bowls that had obviously been turned on a potter's wheel; here on the contrary, they were handmade.... The primitive instrument that did emerge was made of hewn flint. It must belong to the stone age.

Millions of years of evolution were buried under ten feet of clay. The earth was covered with mud. The life on this globe that had pushed its way upward from the fortuitous action of a single spark upon a single cell, to a possible beginning for civilized man, was dead. Or was it? In the same archaeological dig they found, above the ten foot layer of clay, a more sophisticated collection of artifacts. Obviously the marks of a more technically advanced culture. A people who were working with wheels and metals.

If evolution was the only "handle" that man had on the history of his world, what would, quite naturally, be expected above a stone-age culture which had been buried beneath ten feet of clay by a flood[4] covering the whole earth? If we look at this from a point of pure evolution we would be forced to assume that these advanced technicians were descendants, who had somehow escaped the drowning of the earth. The sudden technical advance would need an explanation. This might be justified by the theory that evolution is a many-planed operation; appearing in different states of advancement in different parts of the world. This theory might possibly reduce the area of the flood—and its Biblical history—to one affecting, perhaps, only a small corner of the world.

> Noah's flood may be based upon a real flood that submerged something like 40,000 square miles of the Euphrates Valley sometime between 5400 B.C. and 4200 B.C. The flood wiped out the pre-Sumerians but left some Sumerian cities standing, and their inhabitants repeopled the whole land. (L. Sprague de Camp, *Lost Continents*).

Many of our legends, myths, and historical messages seem to focus on a single catastrophe—a flood. However it has been scientifically recorded that Earth has switched poles possibly four times. The sun has risen in the west and gone down in the east as many times as it has done the reverse. This we find in Egyptian records, the oldest, it is believed, outside of the Tibetan and Sanskrit writings. We have had as many ice ages, and cracking of continents, the changing of land-masses, the sinking of land-masses, the building of mountain ranges—quite possibly because of the shifting of oceanic plates; the birthing of new lands (sometimes by the raising of ocean bottoms and sometimes by the

---

[4] The Chibcha Indians in Columbia claim a deluge was part of the punishment of the god Chibchacun, brought on him by the civilizing teacher, Bochia. Then Bochia opened a hole in the earth and the waters disappeared (*Beginnings: Earth, Sky, Life and Death*, Sophia Lyons Fahs and Dorothy T. Spoerl).

action of volcanoes) and the drowning of older lands. Land has replaced water, and water has replaced land. The Earth that we take for granted today is not the one of that distant past.

Today science is recognizing many of our deep water basins—the Hudson Bay, the Gulf of Mexico, quite possibly the Great Lakes—as probable indications of huge meteor impacts. We now know that comets are a natural part of our world. According to astronomers of today a cloud of comets (the Oort Cloud) orbits the sun. We are now beginning to believe it is quite possible that at least one Earth destruction was caused by a runaway comet. The debris moving between Mars and Jupiter is, in theory, the remains of a destroyed planet. So science tells us. But before science found itself moving into the fields of theology, all creationists held a mighty flood responsible for any and all recognized Earth changes.

The one thing we are fairly convinced of is that Earth man has not had an even-flowing-building-block type of evolution. If what little bit of evidence we have accumulated proves anything at all, it proves that. These are facts we have to deal with. Man's geologic history of Earth gives evidence of a series of destructions. The bones of both man and animal have been broken, mangled, and splintered, by some terrific force; then swept around the world to be found in caves and ravines. Sometimes making up the total composition of whole islands, testifying to massive destruction. Archaeological digs tell the same stories as legend. Geology is now agreeing with archeology and anthropology is saying that these findings are comparable to their own.

Contrary to the smoothly evolving picture we once considered as a factual history of our world, we now know that Earth has fought more than one cataclysmic battle, leaving Earth's readable surface history in such a confused state that every probable answer just poses another question. What we

105

are saying is that this world must have gone through the trauma of birth more than once. Do we find this a logical statement? Can we accept this "more than once" theory within our structured evolutionary frame?

One of the questions I find tantalizing—and one that lies outside this picture of many beginnings—is a simple one. It goes something like this: Can our minds actually conceive of a program by which man, as we see him, can be assembled bit by bit, cell upon cell, bone after bone, to become an individual mover of thought and a personal corporation of soul, mind, and body? Can we logically make the statement that man has acquired that warm, shining part of him that raises him above the animal through a casual association with his own kind lasting a few million years? P.D. Ouspensky offers this explanation (*A New Model of the Universe*):

> In the very beginning in introducing the idea of evolution into biological conception, a bold assumption was made, because without it no theory could be formed. Later it was forgotten that this was only an assumption.

Today we have a confused jumble of hypotheses, theories, opinions, and just plain ideas built around our past and present. These along with a few real facts make up our history. We cling to a mumbo-jumbo mixture of superstition, faith, desire, ritual, and science, that we laboriously drag from generation to generation; treasuring the age and the sentimental value rather than the actual worth of the burden.

We have museums full of bones—both man and animal—about which heavily authorized words are thrust out at us in print, which do not answer any of our questions. All that we have gathered from these bits and pieces is the thought that man today is more uncertain of his origin and his relationship to his world than when he believed the earth was flat. We are learning that everything we "know" is based on knowledge which, in turn, is based on assumptions. And these assumptions are again, in turn, based on a similar "knowing." Our total knowledge structure has a very shaky-foundation.

In looking for positive proof our mathematicians work out extended formulas in a fundamentally correct way, only proving that they are great mathematicians. But like the proverbial "house-of-cards" it-can be, and usually is, dramatically and noisily toppled by a similar "proven" theory.

If we believe that everything has reason and order and all things operate within the jurisdiction of universal law, then evolution might seem to be the logical answer. But—can evolution be presented and affirmed in such a non-diverting manner of cohesive movement that man can find all of himself within its limitations? And we must ask, is evolution a universal law—or is it merely an Earth science?

There are other simpler questions concerning the evolution of society for which we profess to have answers but which still seem to be open to discussion. The easiest of these goes something like this: where did the technological agricultural society spring from about ten thousand years ago?

> In the societies of the Mediterranean basin, there appeared innovators who...brought amazing botanical knowledge that enabled the primitives to transform wild wheat into cultivated wheat by a rational selection of seed. Evidence of that botanical knowledge has been found at Jarmo (Turkey) and Jericho. No satisfactory explanation of the stroke of genius that produced the discovery ten thousand years ago has yet been given....

This information comes from Jean Sendy (*Those Gods Who Made Heaven and Earth*). Does science today have a possible answer? Maybe not. But now I would have to ask why. Why for thousands, maybe millions of years, man is content to be a hunter and forager? And then, for some unknown reason, this free hunter chooses, and seems capable of, taking on the physical and mental tasks of an agricultural society. And then in seemingly quick forward movement we find him working creatively with clay and metals.

It may seem that we are speaking of a very simple operation when we talk about growing things in soil or forming pots from clay, but we have found from experience that it takes a little know-how to have any kind of success with the most basic of plant foods. And as to the pot to cook it in, that could of course be made right from clay, dug up out of the earth—a natural resource—what could be simpler? But clay, even in the hands of an artist, does not become a pot of any kind until it is correctly processed. The processing temperatures used by our modern day potters in their kilns is usually around 1000° C. This business of being a creator of pots, even plain cooking pots, demands some knowledge. Now we ask, did one of our man-animal's (animal-man's) buddies have this kind of knowledge? If so, how did he come by these instructions? Who taught him? And as to the materials one thing puzzles me, how did man discover (learn?) that metals were dug from the earth? Who taught him to recognize them? How many of us today would be able to recognize metals in their natural state?

Archaeological excavations tell us that gold has been a part of early societies for thousands of years. Many ancient civilizations measured the importance of their state by the number of gold artifacts created in their own time. But to create the gold history of these civilizations, first man must be able to recognize the metal in its natural state. Then he has to know how to separate it from the earth. Lastly—and most important for any finished product—he must possess the knowledge for processing this rather sensitive material. Our artists of today process gold under what they claim as low heats. The melting point for gold is something like 1063

C. Was there a fellow member in this new "Society of Man" that knew, had discovered how to melt metals? Who was aware of the temperatures that the different metals required? And had the means to create the temperatures needed for the melting of those metals? In answer to this question here we pose an observation made by P.D. Ouspensky (*A New Model of the Universe*):

> If we trace the amount of intentional, and to a certain degree, conscious work which is necessary to obtain an ordinary knife-blade from a lump of iron ore, we shall never think that a knife-blade could come into being *accidentally*.

If man had had to pick up any part of the science of metallurgy on his own, we should ask, how many generations would have been involved in just the accidental finding and recognizing a source? Let alone acquiring the knowledge for using it creatively through the trial and error method. In other words, how did man, in terms related to natural evolutionary possibilities, pole-vault from a still instinctual caveman into a family-oriented member of society and science? And what is even more questionable—why? What inspired him? Or—why did he find these changes necessary? "Might not life on earth have continued indefinitely without developing intelligence and civilization?" Isaac Asimov asks (*E.T.I.*).

According to professor J.H. Robinson (*The Mind in the Making*), man is not programmed to quite naturally move upward step by step. He has only the potential. He must be educated. He must acquire knowledge through a source. This is the way Professor Robinson tells it:

> We are all born wholly uncivilized. If a group of infants from the best families of today could be reared by apes they would find themselves with no civilization.

Here are a few of the questions those working in these fields of science are asking: Why was the Homo line so successful and what was the moving force that brought it into being? Why did man's ancestor, Homo erectus, exist for millions of years without any significant change, and then quite suddenly, approximately forty-thousand years ago, present a profile of potential modern civilization from which Homo sapien sapien emerged?

Richard E. Leakey (*People of the Lake*) tells us that Rampithecus, our ancient ancestor, was "prowling the forest fringes" between nine and twelve million years ago. And then, he tells us, in the time between nine million years ago and a probable one of four million years ago our fossil history is "as if all life had disappeared from the Earth." The BIG mystery is: what happened on Earth between the four-and-some billion years ago that is the assumed age of Earth, and the four million years ago which is the age of the oldest rocks on Earth's surface? And—the few million years ago that seem to be the evolutionary history of traceable man? Here we might inquire: has our world been just a stage for the constant comings and goings of the various species that have completely disappeared from Earth? Where did they come from? Where did they go?

The passing of our biblical historical figures in their sagas of mythological wanderings has given us a colorful source for speculation, but the stories left behind in stone and bone are the ones we are the most dependent on for our factual evidence. The process of logical reasoning, based on the supportive evidence science has unearthed, along with colorful myths and intuitive probabilities, are all we have on which to construct a past history of man; in turn it might even provide an insight into man's future.

The key—the pieces of that age-old puzzle—lies hidden in sources of legend, mythology, philosophy, ancient histories, rituals, and religions. This key reaches out toward our present day sciences and then curves back into the pagan, the occult—the old persuasions.

I am of the belief that to be nourished only by the lost meanings of the old myths, the sacrificial sterility of a new science, or both, does nothing for the spiritual part of the human who intuitively breathes the beauty of a higher dimensional universe. We can no longer look at man as the ultimate product in a world of Supreme God created forms. Nor can we see him as the non-intelligent-coincidental-happening coming out of a promiscuous marriage between light and algae.

This is a new man. We are looking at a stranger and asking where he came from. Can evolution be seen realistically as the legislator of this biped creature whose inherited instincts keep him an animal? Yet, one who is described as a God-like human, who is endowed with the power to operate on all planes of life. But one who still does not possess the knowledge to recognize those powers within himself?

Old fences are being destroyed. The questionable possibilities of yesterday are the "hard facts" of today. We find it impossible to measure present day phenomena with the same measuring stick that gave us the old truths. Man's love of magic gave us the mythological story of Creation. Man's obsession with bits and pieces, and his need for a whole picture that could be measured according to the old Earth sciences, gave us the sticking-together process called Evolution in which many of the pieces when laid in place do not fit.

Whichever side we speak from, Creation or Evolution, we must accept the probability that close to one-hundred billion human beings, of various sizes and body construction, have, since the Old Stone Age, made Earth their home. Nobody knows where they came from. But, however little we know about them, we have archaeological evidence that fifteen thousand years ago a human skull was left in Texas. A human died at the southern tip of South America ten thousand years ago and at the same time, a few thousand miles to the north, in what is now called Nevada, man left his mark, while twelve thousand years ago we might find man tracking the great mammoth in the state of New Mexico.

From the excavation of Shanidar Cave in Iraq we pick up dates of seven-thousand, twelve-thousand, and thirty-four thousand, with one hundred thousand years at the fourth level, about forty-five feet down. There are signs at that depth of there having been, in that period, extreme cold and wetness. The three skeletons found at the forty-five foot level were Neanderthal man.

Many poetic and flowery explanations of that spiritually motivated individual called Man have been around for a long time. Most of our beliefs have been formed around a small mythical and physical perspective. But the propagating forces that bring our physical world into being are not in themselves physical. Our Ancients tell us they flow down-ward from a high source. They are the creator of all life—the builder of worlds.

With the splitting of the atom man discovered the universal force. We seem to be quite sure of this. With the splicing of genes from physical organisms man has uncovered the secret life-pattern within which the universal force constructs its life-forms. Of this we are positive. Man now holds the key to all life including his own.

> ...all living material is, by this, reduced to simply
> an arrangement of chemicals. (Sharon Kathleen
> McAuliffe, *Life for Sale*).

The door to this new science now stands open. Genetic engineering is about to turn our familiar world upside down. The emergence of Man and Earth out of nothing is unacceptable today within our scientific society. We are inclined to be objectively skeptical as to Man and his world falling within the jurisdiction of a magician's rabbit-out-of-a-hat trick. This, we are sure, does not explain Man's beginning.

> ...colonization, not evolution, may be the major factor in the spread of life in the universe. (*Colony: Earth*, Richard E. Mooney).

Copernicus, Newton, and Galileo were responsible for the realization that our Earth is not the center of the universe. The stars were not put into our heavenly skies for the pure beautification of our lives. Darwin made us look at the probability of a beginning for Man other than the one brought about mystically and mythically by a benevolent God. And he speculated that the time required for the emergence of Man as a species was more likely hundreds of thousands of years of evolution. Man was much older than Creation allowed. With the appearance of biological engineering as a reality, today one is tempted to explore this question of beginning from a new and, at first glance, perhaps bizarre perspective.

Is it possible, we ask, that both the theories of creation and evolution—with the supporting data, fossil finds, legends, and history—are only partial explanations for human existence? And what if linked together by the scientific miracles of current and projected techniques, they become metaphorical thirds of the puzzle? Perhaps right here we should ask this question: Were man's gods universal beings? Was man genetically "created?"

The millennia passed—to the Anunnaki each 3,600 years was but one year of their own cycle—they began to complain. Spacemen should not be ask
to work in dark, dusty mines. A mutiny was declared, the Anunnaki left the mines and burned their tools. Anu came down to Earth and decided that the mining operation must be discontinued but Ea offered a solution to the problem of

workers. In southeastern Africa a life-form had evolved that could be trained to perform some of the mining tasks—the apemen and the apewomen—if only the "mark of the Anunnaki" could be put upon them. Ea was given permission to "create a Lulu," a "primitive worker who would bear the yoke of the Anunnaki."⁵

---

⁵ *The Stairway to Heaven* by Zecharia Sitchin: "The Akkadians called them Llu, 'Lofty Ones' from which the Hebrew biblical El stems. The Canaanites and Phoenicians called them *Ba'al*, Lord. But at the very beginning of all these religions, the Sumerians called them DIN.GIR, 'the Righteous Ones of the Rocketships.'"

GENETIC ENGINEERING

STATUTE 35 U.S.C. S101:

Whoever invents or discovers any new and useful process, machine, manufacture or composition of matter, or any new and useful improvement thereof, may obtain a patent therefore.

June 1980—The Supreme Court ruled that man-made organisms could be patented.

THE MIAMI HERALD, Friday, Dec. 5 1980

Patent Given for Cloning Method

STANFORD, Calif.—(UP) The U.S. Patent Office has issued a patent for a gene splicing and cloning method developed by scientists at Stanford and the University of California in San Francisco, say Stanford officials.

The inventors of the gene cloning technique are Dr. Stanley N. Cohen of Stanford and Dr. Herbert W. Boyer of U.C. San Francisco.

Their research created the field of research known as recombinant DNA. Within months, experiments involving the cloning of bacterial and animal cell DNA from various sources were being carried out in a number of laboratories. These procedures have enabled studies of the organization of complex chromosomes in ways not possible previously.

In the past decade, gene cloning has become increasingly sophisticated, and the promise of the technique has given rise to a multimillion-dollar gene cloning industry.

The first cloning undertaken with sophisticated technology was in 1952. Doctors Robert Briggs and Thomas J. King of the Institute for Cancer Research in Philadelphia replaced the nucleus of an already fertilized frog egg with a tissue of another frog not of the same species. The tadpoles were exact copies of the tissue-cell donor.

Man was, and in many minds still is, seen as a creation—the created image of God. But then those bright inspirational miracles of Creation were confronted by the pragmatically scientific and intriguing movement of Evolution. Man was not a creation. Man had come into this world accidentally—or coincidentally, and evolved gradually and naturally through millions of years.

Today the parlayers of magic and miracles unearth and bring forth into the light of understanding, a professed new but in actuality very old gift of the Magi—the biological creation of man through the science of genetics. Scientific creation. But who were the creators? In this chapter we are asking: is genetic engineering—scientific creation—a thing out of man's past? Is man an engineered form with god-person connections? Is man only a very small part of a vast universally engineered celestial world? Has man's millions of years of evolution been spent moving in a circle giving the impression that man is now, with the discovery of genetic engineering, arriving right back at his beginning? And does man now possess the knowledge, the courage, and the curiosity to create a higher form of life—in his image? To become as gods?

Man has moved forward searching for himself, slowly feeling his way. Stumbling like a blind man over the unrelenting premise of a static, orderly world, supervised and controlled by God. Seeking a beginning and a meaning for a thing called "Life." Maybe somewhere in the dark recesses of the mind an ancient memory urged him on. He began recognizing himself when Hippocrates (460-357 B.C.) in ancient Greece began the study of the human body; it was through him that man discarded a former belief that disease was due to a vengeful god.

Then Galen (A.D. 136-210) furthered man's understanding of himself by the discovery of two sets of nerves and proof that arteries contained blood. Then in the seventeenth century Fabricus (1537-1619) made the discovery that veins had valves, and Harvey (1578-1657) found the mechanics behind the circulation of blood. All of these were very important discoveries. But—two thousand years before these revelations the Chinese Book of Medicine (*Neiching*) had this to say:

> All the blood of the human body is under the control of the heart and regulated by it. The blood flows continuously in a circle and never stops; it cannot but flow ceaselessly like the current of a river or the sun and the moon in their courses.

The western man of "modern" science was not aware of this. He continued his slow climb upward; Malpighe (1628-1694) made the discovery that there were air cells in the lungs and Bicha (1771-1802) studied tissue and parts of human organs. Then in the nineteenth century a German scientist, T. Schwann, proved that all animals were strictly a composition of cells, and an Austrian monk, Gregor Mendel, through his famous experiments with peas, established the law of genetics. But this was not recognized until nearly one hundred years later.

There are many names unheralded and unacknowledged, that should be given credit for playing an important role in the drama of man's agelong attempt to understand himself. There were many tinkerers and seekers; not all were scientists. And many experiments were performed by these curious minds that did not produce the "desired" results, but many of these can be considered "fortunate accidents" as they proved to be beneficial to all mankind. By the beginning of the twentieth century, man was familiar with the benevolent creator of the human species—the nucleic acids. And in 1953 the probability of an artificially induced higher form of animal life suddenly became a part of our modern science through the discovery of the DNA (deoxyribonucleic acid)[6] structure by the team of James Dewey Watson, an American, and Francis Crick, of Britain.

Watson and Crick were actually just a jump ahead of some of their fellow scientists; they were the first to unveil a three-dimensional structure showing the DNA as a double molecule in the form of a helix. This was eagerly accepted by those in the field of biology as a long step forward in the solution to the mystery of man and his beginning. By the 1960s geneticists had learned to read the DNA code and within a period of only a few decades they had produced evidence to show that the necessary building blocks of a cell can be constructed out of simple ordinary compounds found in any science lab. This is the breakdown:

The DNA structure has four bases: adenine(A), thynine (T), guanine(G), and cystonine(C). The four bases are attached to a sugar molecule in the backbone of the DNA molecule chain. According to Watson and Crick the DNA molecule is something like a spiral staircase—the phosphate and sugars forming the twisting railing of the stairs and the bases forming the steps. Each step is composed of two bases joined in the middle and always in pairs. Adenine always joins with thynine to form a step and guanine always joins with cystonine. The steps may follow each other endlessly and in order such as AT, GC, AT, CG, TA, TA, etc. "When the chromosomes duplicate themselves the whole DNA

---

[6] A basic material in the chromosomes of the cell nucleus; it contains the genetic code and transmits the hereditary pattern.

stairway comes apart in the middle in a kind of unzipping motion."

This is the way that Watson and Crick describe it. "All of the As separate from the Ts, and the Gs separate from the Cs. Then each half of the stairway grows a new half, picking its raw material from the cell contents around it." Geneticists now believe that different personalities are brought about by the different arrangements of the TAs, ATs, CGs, and GCs; and we have been told that if a single cell was unwound it might be found to contain as many as one million genes. Now that is rather mind-boggling! And, a single gene, our geneticists tell us, could be a "chunk" of DNA "stairway" perhaps as much as two thousand steps long. Then we have to remember that all of this is only a part of a very tiny cell which Webster describes as "the smallest vital element." In keeping with this Watson and Crick see this small vital element as an advanced electronic feedback system; functioning like a modern computer; programmed for corrections— or changes, and capable of an independent existence.

We are told that the cell works with three different kinds of RNA (ribonucleic acid)—mRNA, tRNA, and rRNA. RNA is described as looking like "half of a twisted ladder" and it differs from DNA only in its sugar, which is ribose, having more oxygen atoms in its molecule than the deoxyribose of DNA. The coded information that is carried in the molecules of DNA are the instructions needed by the cells in order to produce protein. On this DNA and RNA[7] seem to work together: supposedly DNA acts as the master planner while RNA takes the secondary position of a contractor.

According to the information we possess today, here is the way it is proposed to work. A DNA segment about to

---

[7] An essential component of all living matter, present in the Cytoplasm of all cells and comprised of long chains of phosphate and sugar ribose along with several bases. One form is the carrier of genetic information from the nuclear DNA and is important in the synthesis of proteins in the cell.

order a supply of proteins operates this way: with the assistance of enzymes and available building blocks it "stamps out" a string of messenger RNA (mRNA). This messenger moves out into the cytoplasm, the cell's factory area. The transfer RNA (tRNA), in the meantime, has attached itself to the amino acids in the cytoplasm, intent on delivering them to the ribosomes and matching them up to the mRNA.

The way I understand it, the meeting of the rRNA and ribosome is necessary before the protein-synthesizing process can begin. When the materials—the amino acids—have been delivered by tRNA and matched up to the instructions delivered by the mRNA, the protein is manufactured and on completion is released by the ribosomes to go out and do its job of building and reproducing, accurately most of the time.

Occasionally errors occur, but our "computerized" cells are mostly programmed for quick repair. However, the repair of inaccurate reproduction depends on the retention of the original sequential pattern for comparative instructions; if the initial pattern is lost the error becomes part of a new design, a mutation which will become a part of all future copies. We might be able to lay the blame for error on the third RNA—rRNA (Ribosoma). This form of RNA is believed to be in charge of organizing the sequence of amino acids in the chain. However, recently our researchers have discovered that the "genetic code of the higher organisms is sometimes interrupted by ostensibly nonsensical, meaningless segments of DNA." They seem to be instructions that were never carried out. Somehow, somewhere along the line the pattern had been changed. And in keeping with this there are mutated and powerless genes lazing around in the system, collecting into something resembling a "junkyard." These same researchers have witnessed another phenomenon, a "jumping gene"[8] which cannot be accounted for. This is a gene whose antics include choreographing its own moves, changing information, and turning neighboring genes off and on and destroying man's picture of the body operating like a well-oiled mechanism. Science Vol. 263 . 4 February 1994 "Talkin' Trash: a Glossary of Junk DNA."

Many geneticists, uncertain about what to make of this apparently superfluous DNA, have taken to referring to it as "junk." But what looks like junk can hide gems, and there is new and growing evidence that some junk DNA may be of great value....

In the early 1970s a technique was developed for splitting the DNA molecule by means of enzymes. After splitting the DNA, researchers found that they could snip out certain parts and splice these to the DNA of another cell or virus. This is called Recombinant DNA. Recombinant DNA is the creative process through which new lifeforms are "born." This creation is merely a manipulation of bases in the DNA. The procedure for the creation of new life-forms is, we are told, exceedingly simple. Ted Howard and Joshua Rifkin (*Who Should Play God?*) tell us:

> ...recombinant DNA is a kind of biological sewing machine that can be used to stitch together the genetic fabric of unrelated organisms. ...a chemical scalpel, called a restriction enzyme, is used to split apart the DNA molecule from one source—a human, for example. Once the DNA has been cut into pieces a small segment of genetic material—a gene perhaps, or a few genes at length—is separated out. Next the restriction enzyme is used to slice out a segment from the body

---

[8] Genes are DNA sequences that either carry the information for making proteins or play some other direct role in protein synthesis (such as making the transfer RNAs that help assemble amino acids into proteins). But in higher species, the overwhelming majority of the DNA—97% in humans—does not code for proteins or RNAs with clear functions.

of a plasmid, a short length of DNA found in bacteria. Both the pieces of human DNA and the body of the plasmid develop "sticky ends" as a result of the slicing process. The ends of both segments of DNA are then hooked together forming a genetic whole composed of materials from the two Original sources. Finally, the modified plasmid is used as a vector, or vehicle, to move the DNA into a host cell, usually a bacteria. Absorbing the plasmid, the bacterium proceeds to duplicate it endlessly, producing identical copies of the chimera. That is called a clone.

The business of snipping and adding or exchanging parts covers the fields of medicine, pharmacology, agriculture, food processing, mining, and the manufacture of artificial chemicals, to name a few. This future carries a promise of unlimited possibilities. Biological experiments are proving the importance of this method in the making of liquids and gases; almost anything can be converted into a combustible fuel by the introduction of a bacteria, they say.

In the field of medicine biogenetic engineers are now developing vaccines and hormones for animals as well as for humans. Recently, by copying short sections of proteins and parts of disease viruses, researchers have succeeded in synthesizing experimental vaccines for hepatitis, diphtheria, and other diseases. I have recently read an article on "Monoclonal Antibody Therapeutics in Development" appearing in the *Scientific American*, July of 1993, making the statement that throughout the next decade, dozens of bio-technological firms will "struggle to turn monoclonal antibodies (MABS) harvested from mouse tumors into new drugs." These new drugs will treat everything from cancer to bacterial infections. Today we have Idec Pharmaceuticals and Immunomedics, two firms researching cures for bluell lymphoma working through phases 1-2-3. (The phases have to do with the different steps taken in seeking the marketing approval of the Food and Drug Administration). Another firm, NeoRx, is working with the Murine Antibodies (MABS) in the development of a remedy for breast and ovarian cancer. Does this sound exciting? Interesting? Or would you rather get back to that old reliable, aspirin?

Many of us believe that bioengineering, even in its infancy, is to become an important part of our world today. But amazing things are promised for the more distant tomorrows by those working in this new field. Here are a few of the "miracles" we can expect to be a part of our life style eventually. We may logically assume that there will be a variety of biochemicals produced, such as antibiotics and hormones, perhaps enzymes that can convert sunlight directly into food substances—or usable energy. And it's possible that it will be genetically feasible to be able to choose the color of our hair— eyes—or skin. And change our behavioral patterns and upgrade our intelligence. How smart would you like to be? And what kind of a body would you like to own? Short? Tall? Pleasantly-plump? Skinny? How about somewhere in between with all curves in the right places?

From what I understand there will be body shops, much like our beauty salons of today, where the human form can be cosmetically updated for a price. But then there will also be body shops for the more serious repairs of damaged parts; entirely new members will be artificially grown. Genetic engineering can be seen as our future creator—or recreator of all life forms. Tomorrow's magic genie. Just make a wish. "If one knows the grammar, one can begin to make up new sentences." So says Michael Rogers (*The DNA Story,* Watson & Tooze). "Dial-a-baby, then? Or better, dial-a-monster? Not by a long shot, yet. The brand-new techniques work, thus far, only with bacteria and viruses...."

In 1959 Richard Feynman, a physicist at the California Institute of Technology, gave a talk in which he made the statement that he saw the "world of molecules as a potential building site for all sorts of new structures," where tiny devices created to perform specific tasks could be built. "We can imagine building tiny 'cities' with industries that produce specific molecular-sized instruments. Infinitesimal computers could control this molecular world. Molecular societies could be constructed for human ends. The micro world is a realm as vast as outer space." (*The Cosmic Code,* Heinz R. Pagels)

Forrest Carter of the Naval Research Laboratory is looking to genetic engineering for "electronic devices." Small duplicating organic computers, tiny enough to "live inside the bloodstream or the brain." He sees this as a future aid to medicine. Kevin M. Ulmer, of the Maryland Genex Corporation, talks about synthetic genes that will be engineered to attack only diseased cells. EANTECH's Martin Apple believes that it might be possible to develop a protein that would be directly responsible for "revitalization of a nervous system;" and which might, quite possibly, become a source of "growth stimulation" for missing parts of the body.

George Kenyon of the University of California sees a "minuscule supercomputer" giving man a third set of teeth. There are those who picture a whole customized life form specifically designed to fit a particular niche in life, commercial or social. In the labor market there would probably be a demand for workers to fill the needs of manufacturing and processing plants, but those catering to the social needs might receive an order reading something like this:

Please fill in the color of skin, eyes and hair with each order. Size = tall (T), medium (M), short (S). Instructions for personality implementation included with all orders.				
ITEM #	SEX	DESCRIPTION	SIZE	QTY
1234 B	*M*	*Social Escort*	*T*	*1*
		Send replacement for 1234 A. Not good in tux. Sexually uncoordinated.		

COLOR & COLOR NUMBER					
SKIN	**#**	**EYES**	**#**	**HAIR**	**#**
White	*1*	*Blue*	*2*	*Black*	*3*

Payment: Visa, American Express, MasterCard

Account # _____

Signature _____

Those of us who have cut our teeth on the Sears and Roebuck catalogue will have no problem with this. But why not order a whole army—or navy? An armed force made to order?

The discovery of DNA forced man to look at himself in an entirely different way; life—he must now acknowledge— is a chain of chemical reactions. All life is matter. Man is matter and all matter is made up of cells, and every cell is a library of instructions by which these cells are constructed and organized, then motivated to produce their own likeness.

Man is now in the business of divining the method by which he can change, or reproduce these cells within the human body as easily as he does in a laboratory. Now that he has the know-how, all he needs is the courage to take on the new role of "Creator." Joshua Lederberg, of the California Institute of Technology, makes this statement: "...we might manage such tinkering with heredity in ten or twenty years." But according to Doctor Carl Berkley from the Medical Research Engineering we hear: "...on the basis of the present technical knowledge we could right now produce a system which would meet the basic criteria for life."

Cetus, based in Berkeley, California, is the biggest and the oldest of the firms (1970) to have come out of molecular biology. Genentech (Genetic Engineering Technology) was the first company to give the public a chance to buy stock in a DNA corporation. When Genentech went public in September 1980, its shares jumped in a matter of minutes, from $35.00 to $89.00.

At the time of my research between 1970 and 1980, the United States government had given out two hundred DNA research grants. There was believed to be, at that time, 200,000 biologists in the world, with eighty research laboratories, seven major pharmaceutical companies, and twice that many chemical and agricultural corporations following this intensely interesting and lucrative parade of progress. At that time the United States Patent Office had allowed General Electric to take out three such patents in this new field while Wall Street investment firms watched impatiently, waiting for the DNA monster to grow into lucrative monetary opportunities. It hit like a huge tidal wave. In 1976 Stephen Turner founded the Bethesda Research Laboratories and within a year's time had sold $100,000 worth of restriction enzymes, this figure has now grown to more than $2.5 million.

If you find this interesting and if you are a do-it-yourself hobbyist, here is one for you—at the firm Toronto Biologicals for the approximate price of one of our better new automobiles (BMW) one can purchase a "gene-machine." Biologicals makes the claim that with a thirty-minute crash course in its operation any intelligent human will be able to create his (or her) own new life forms. Or—if you are already into that and you are now in the market for a viral DNA, some infected tissues, culture cells, or a few cubic centimeters of restriction enzymes, you can order all these and more from a gene-splicing supply company. I wonder if this is the way Dr. Frankenstein got started. New toys for future boys? Are we loosing a monster on the world, a thing nightmares are made of?

The recent discoveries in the field of genetics have thrust upon a few of our own species the power to tamper with life in such a way as to bring into being totally unpredictable life forms for which we may not be prepared mentally, physically or socially. For this reason the International Conference on Recombinant DNA Molecules was held at Asilomar, California, in 1975, to establish guidelines within which biological studies could feel free to operate.

However, in 1976, the National Institute of Health formed a Recombinant DNA molecule program establishing more firmly the guidelines for operation. Government regulations now have these levels of classification for biological experiments: Pl, which is thought of as having no unnatural or harmful possibilities contained within the specimens; P2 is something that would be considered a possible low risk, but is understood by the biologists today; P3 falls into the category of either a high potential of possible contamination or a field that biologists are not familiar with; and P4 would be something that is completely unknown as to specimen and possible result and would be considered a high risk experiment.

Our history tells us that the alchemists dreamed of creating life. Paracelsus proposed a technique involving human semen and blood. This mixture, with the right amount of nurturing warmth and a correct "aging" period, would, it was believed, produce a "true living infant." Although much smaller than a human child at birth, it would eventually grow to the size of an average adult. This creation was thought of as a "homunculus." That was yesterday. Today Professor Tribe (Harvard Law School) tells us:

> Genetic engineering is one of the new technolo-
> gies that could be responsible for altering the
> very meaning of humanity.

All our material on this new art of creation tells us that our future life may be something that can be designed—or redesigned—and no modification will be outside the technical talents of the new biologist; new forms may be artificially grown in a lab or "manufactured" from another organism. In this way the "perfect man" may be born. This has always been the idealistic vision of the Eugenics "cult," the only difference being that they saw it coming about through "proper breeding." This new technology seems to make that envisioned Utopia a definite possibility.

There are those who dreamily anticipate Man's mystical evolution through the art of genetic engineering. There are many others who wait anxiously for that perfected species that will be the answer to all commercial needs; employers will put in an order for employees much as they would for a new machine.

Many scientists claim it is possible even at this stage of the game to "upgrade" an animal's intelligence to that of a nine-to-five worker. Professor Lederberg believes that the first step will be to "implant human cell nuclei into animals and thus produce hybrids." We would like to inquire along with Martin Ebon (*The Cloning of Man*), "How far would parahuman reproduction techniques be advanced?" Particularly in a scientific world that has not always been guided by ethical considerations. In answer we hear this from John Bass (*Government Control Research in Positive Genetics*):

> ...the government might be confronted with the
> problem of arbitrarily classifying the progeny of
> unsuccessful clones which are to be killed, or as
> humanoids, who will be permitted to live at the
> government's expense as a reminder of the imper-
> fect operation of cloning techniques.

Sounds like science fiction? That's our future. Out of the past we have this: the Brahman writings of India tell us that divine spacemen performed biological experimentations with apes. That is what our ancient records tell us. But here is an interesting item that I picked up from a local paper, *The Miami News*. It is dated November 12, 1982:

> Recently, an otherwise normal baby was born with a two-inch tail. The tail had hair and nerves but no bone or cartilage. It was removed by routine surgery. Such occurrences are rare but hardly unknown.

Man is, our science tells us, the product of an engineered program, DNA. He is, in a sense, his own creator. And quite possibly will be in the future, the creator of others—replicas of himself. His image. If this is so we might ask, could this all have happened before? Is this a very old script, played on the same stage, with just a change of cast?

Maybe the source of our mythical, theoretical history can be found in the natural appearance of a biped animal in a newly colonized—maybe reconstructed world. To follow this script our gods were, quite possibly, men of science who became scientifically interested in the strange walking beasts (which would explain the stories of man mating with animals).

Maybe it was just plain old-fashioned curiosity that compelled them to take that first step—the computerization of the brain of a biped animal—the beginning of a new species called "human" (which would explain the stories about the gods mating with the daughters of man). Maybe we are a race created or seeded and tended by others of our universal world (that might explain the mysterious Flying Saucers). And maybe Adam (or Adade, or Atum, or any of the other names he is known by) was the image of his creator, a clone.

Perhaps Eve *did* come to life through the removal of Adam's rib. Possibly, as in surgery today, the removal of the rib was for the purpose of easy access to the internal organs of bisexual Adam. The separation of male and female. Here, from Z'ev ben Shimon Halevi (*Kabbalah*) comes a bit of ancient religious philosophy:

> The World of Yezirah was the Garden of Eden[9] where the androgynous...man created in Beriah (Genesis 1:27) was separated into Adam and Eve in clearly differentiated male and female reflections of the outer Pillars.

The field of genetic engineering carries our official science into the never-never land of our ancient stories. The process has to do with the manipulation of genes which will, according to our information, create entirely new life-forms. Man? Animal-man? Meta-man?

Horticulturists had, for a long time, been able to grow a living plant—the exact image of the parent plant—from just a small piece of the "mother plant," a cutting. Then man's mind began to question the possibility of reproduction of one of its own kind from a similar "cutting." Why not, they were asking. Today, all over the globe, small god-like humans anticipate a future of man-made creations. Maybe in man's mental, experience-keyed library, among the ancient and dusty memoirs of other lives, a small, quiet voice is leading him right back to where he came from.

The history of Man is a labyrinth of dark passages, sometimes leading nowhere and at other times into an even deeper maze; entering our world at strange times and in unexpected places. But this same doorway that opens into our world today, out of a passage of millions of years (a few

---

[9] "Eden, or the Hebrew Gan-Eden, meaning the park or the garden of Eden, is an archaic name of the country watered by the Euphrates and its many branches, from Asia and Armenia to the Erythraian Sea."

civilizations, and many catastrophes) must have, logically, at one time, opened outward from a new world toward a new life.

Every step we take along the path of factual scientific discovery allows another piece of that ancient jig-saw puzzle to fall into place. Like a universal game of chess, man takes a new position on the gameboard moving one step at a time, taking into consideration where he has been as related to where he now stands and allowing this information to influence his direction. Pawn or king he is motivated, persuaded, or pushed by the magic of imagination and the spirit of curiosity.

Yesterday, the bright, inspirational, miracles of Creation were overshadowed by the pragmatically intriguing movement of Evolution. Today's scientific parlayers of magic and miracles unearth and bring forth into the light of day a professed new but really very old "gift of the Magi"—the creation of Man. We are now in a similar position to that ancient serpent who found it necessary to grasp his own tail between his teeth. We have reached that place in the life of mankind where man (again?) possesses the knowledge and courage needed to create a higher form of life. Edgar Cayce tells it this way:

> Accordingly, the Sons of God set themselves to working at creation also and fashioned or evolved the flesh bodies which were intended to be channels for man's eventual release from his material being...through the glandular centers of the higher developed species of primates that were chosen as the most advantageous of the animals then inhabiting the earth....

Subject for thought: Science Fiction? Could this be possible? This picture of our beginning comes from the mind of Walter Ernstine in *The Day the Gods Died*. Could this be possible?

The truth is that 40,000 years ago the Alturians captured diverse hominid groups in South Africa, the Sahara, in northern Europe, and in Mongolia. Then the aliens subjected their captives to the process of transforming their genes—by changing the sequence of bases in the DNA macromolecule, the Alturian scientists cultivated artificial genes in their laboratories. After the growth of the programmed chain of chromosomes was complete, they were used for artificial insemination by introducing this "sperm" directly into the uterus of female hominids. (Immaculate conception?) The males of the primitive species were rendered sterile by exposing them to properly adjusted doses of radiation. They could continue to indulge in their sexual drive and believe the new-born off-spring to be their own. This had the advantage that the male hominids would protect their mates as well as their young from all dangers of the environment. Eventually these new-born—and also mutated—young ones became fertile.

The experiments were discontinued after four decades as soon as the results proved positive. The new breed of Cro-Magnon man was already far more intelligent as a child than any adult Neanderthal man. The galactic Medical Council called back its representatives, for they were needed in other worlds.

The only trace of the Alturian research expedition that stayed behind on Earth was a small control base. It was completely automatic, radioing its report to the control council at regular intervals. The control base also checked the activity of warning probes which orbited around the planet as artificial satellites. The probes' special mission was to warn any spaceship belonging to

the Galactic Federation away from landing on
Earth. Any intervention—however insignificant it
might be—into the further development of the
successfully mutated new species of man was
strictly forbidden.

...Nearly 20,000 years went by.

Then—

An illegal emigrant space ship of the Alturians
landed on earth.

The Hubble Space Telescope,
designed to record images of very faint objects at great
distances.

5

GODS AND SPACE

From Miami Herald, Oct. 1982

'They are visiting us at a time when our technology is at a stage where theirs was hundreds of years back in their history' said Charles Kubokawa. Thus, they are from the *future* in the sense that it will probably be hundreds of years before we reach the same level of technology,' Kubokawa explained.

'They could be from within the earth because we really haven't looked every place. Three-quarters of the earth is covered with water and we have never explored very much under water,' Kubokawa (a NASA employee for 15 years) pointed out.

The search for intelligent life in parts of the universe other than that part called "Earth" is entering an era of respectability. New discoveries and new ways of searching for our cosmic neighbors are exciting physicists like Dr. Philip Morrison and Dr. Giuseppi Cocconi at MIT (Massachusetts Institute of Technology). Out of this interest came a commission, created for the express purpose of dealing with the search for extraterrestrial intelligence (SETI). The prospect of such a search is overwhelming, but intriguing, although to some it is something to be filed away in a dark corner under the stamp of "impossible." A NASA budget of $1.5 million yearly gives a certain amount of authority and prestige to those in the impossible business of locating other civilizations.

I like to think that by now we should be fairly certain that other civilizations do exist. Right? Also, by all the evidence that we of the planet Earth, in our own primitive way, have brought to light, we must assume that these other civilizations are much older than our own. Right?

Now by our own small bit of logic, it would seem obvious that these older and higher forms of civilization would be very active—as we are—and curious as we are— plus more scientifically advanced, so we must assume that there would not be too much happening in their universe that they were not aware of. So, again, if this supposition is to be taken as a possible truth, then we should also suppose that these other civilizations are quite familiar with all happenings on the blue planet called Earth. Right? This is the way it looks to me.

By now I am assuming that visitors from space played an important role in the construction of Earth and the birth of humanity. The Ancient Ones called those visitors by different names, but all saw them as "those who come from above." Perhaps they are still watching over us, and, perhaps this would be an explanation for the presence of the mysterious flying saucers that have been added to our list of "impossibles."

The scientific part of our established civilization is not enthusiastically seeking explanations for the strange, silent spacecraft that have become a part of our lives. Maybe that is because they have an inner conviction that if they acknowledge the existence of UFOs there will be the need to do something about them—now that might be a real impossibility. Who would want to be standing in those shoes? Perhaps it is as rumors have it—our government has already had meetings with our extraterrestrial neighbors, something they are filing as "highly sensitive material."

In 1951 our own United States government established an investigative office, Project Blue Book, at the Wright Patterson Air Force Base in Dayton, Ohio, to study the many "flying saucer" reports that were being received from citizens and the Air Force pilots. Many of the investigators admit to dealing with "interesting cases" which even today remain in the files unexplained. Many cases were considered "classified" and no information on them was given out to the public. The public was given only surface explanations on many of those investigated and strongly discouraged from any private investigations. In the last twenty-five years, especially since Project Blue Book closed its doors in 1969, many individuals have spent their own time and money gathering data on these strange "hallucinatory" sightings that are still being reported. These investigators now have findings that show this has been going on for many hundreds of years.

We hear this from Jacques Vallée (*The Invisible College*).

> Scientific curiosity has led to the first international conference on extraterrestrial civilizations and the problem of contact with them.

Apparently the event was held in September of 1971. The event was organized jointly by the highly respected U.S. National Academy of Sciences and the U.S.S.R. Academy of Sciences along with scientists from several other nations participating and was held in Soviet Armenia:

> The subjects of discussion focused on the origin of life on Earth, the origin and evolution of intelligence, and particularly the possibilities of life on other cosmic bodies and the problem of searching for, and possible consequences of establishing contact with these extraterrestrial civilizations.

Ten years previously, this had taken place in South America:

> The Inter-American Bar Association Bogota, Colombia (1961):
>
> *Magna Carta of Space*, submitted by William Hyman, Part ll, Interplanetary Affairs—
>
> That in the event it proves there are intelligent beings on any other world, their sovereignty shall be recognized and their laws respected by all peoples of this Earth. That aggression or conquest or warfare of any kind shall never be waged by any earthly nation or group of nations against any other inhabited world in the Solar System. That Earth shall carry on a peace policy throughout the universe.

Earth's human has allowed himself to become aware of this phenomenon and let it move into his thinking processes only since he has discovered that he, quite possibly, does possess the technical knowledge that will allow him to visit worlds other than his own. His graduation into this type of thinking was brought on by that "one giant step" on the moon. Regardless of all this there are still some posturing authoritative figures who would like to assume that what is being seen is some illusive thing called swamp gas, or low flying weather balloons—or even high flying pterodactyl. Any of these would set better with them than the sighting of a UFO. In spite of this we are still getting reports from some very esteemed sources:

We have these reports from our astronauts regarding strange ships that follow them—sometimes seeming to play games, operating as if they wanted to be recognized:

- February 20, 1962: John Glenn, Mercury capsule flight. *Three UFOs followed him.*
- May 24, 1962. Scott Carpenter, Mercury VII. Photographs taken by Carpenter of UFO he saw.

138

- May 30, 1962: Joe Walton, X15. Photograph taken by Walton of five UFOs.
- July 17, 1962: Robert White, X15. White photographed several UFOs.
- May 16, 1963: Gordon Cooper, Mercury VIII. Cooper saw a green UFO, also tracked by radar on the ground.
- October 3, 1963: Walter Schirra, Mercury IX. Schirra reported several UFOs.
- March 8, 1964: Russia Voshkod II. One UFO reported.
- June 3, 1964: Jim McDivitt, Gemini IV. McDivitt photographed several UFOs.
- November 14, 1969: Apollo XII. Conrad, Bean, and Gordon reported a UFO that followed them from Earth to within 130,000 miles of the moon.[1]

We get this from our government offices:

> These instructions were prepared by the consultants panel to the United States Air Force.
> IF YOU SEE A UFO WHAT SHOULD YOU DO? Remain calm and objective. Then:
> 1. Write down everything that you can observe, or what you can remember, if it is a brief sighting.
> 2. If a camera is available, use it to photograph what you see. Include reference points in your shots so that later the object can be analyzed in the context of its surroundings.
> 3. Draw a picture of what you see as accurately as possible, again indicating reference points and size relationships.
> 4. If other witnesses are available, get them to substantiate what you saw by drawing and writing down exactly what they saw.

---

[1] This is only a partial list taken from *The Edge of Reality* authored by J. Allen Hynek and Jacques Vallée, Regnery: Chicago, 1975.

5. If there is any physical evidence left by the UFO, immediately seal off the area and make note of what was left in evidence. If possible, containerize it to the best of your ability. The samples you take may be dirt, shrubs, rocks, or any item that may have been affected.
6. If you encounter an extraterrestrial being:

a. Do not approach the being.

b. Photograph it, if possible.

c. Try to keep the subject in sight.

d. Try to keep out of sight of the subject.

e. If you are approached, do not fight or act aggressive. All indications point to the fact that past contacts have been friendly.

Portion of memo from Director of Naval Intelligence:

INFO: (e) Director of Naval Intelligence, Navy Department, Washington 25, D.C.

(f) Commander Eastern Sea Frontier, 90 Church Street, New York, 7, N.Y.

(g) Commandant, Potomac River Naval Command, U.S. Naval Gun Factory, Washington 25, D.C.

b. The symbol FLYOBRPT [Flying Object Report] will appear at the beginning of the text of messages to facilitate identification.

c. Reports will include, insofar as possible:

(I) A brief description of the object(s); shape. size, color, number, formation if more than one, aerodynamic features, trail or exhaust, propulsion system speed. sound. maneuvers, manner of disappearance, and other permanent or unusual features.

(2) Time of sighting in 24-hour clock zonal time, and length of time observed.

(3) Manner of observation; visual or electronic, from air (give speed. altitude, and

type of aircraft) or surface. Any type of optical or electronic equipment used should be described.

(4) Location of observer during sighting, giving exact latitude and longitude as closely as feasible, and/or reference to a known landmark. Location of object(s) with respect to observer, giving distance, direction, and altitude.

(5) Identifying information of observer(s) and witness(s), estimate of reliability and experience, and any factor bearing on estimated reliability of the sighting.

(6) Weather and winds aloft conditions at time and place of sighting(s).

(7) Any activity or condition, meteorological or otherwise, which might account for the sighting.

(8) Existence of any physical evidence such as fragments, photographs and the like, of the sighting.

(9) Interception or identification action taken. (Such action may be taken whenever feasible, complying with existing air defense directives).

(10) Location of any air traffic in the general area at the time of the sighting.

d. It should be noted that the above instructions are separate from those required for reporting normal surface and air sightings prescribed by reference (b) and CINCLANTFLT instructions concerning same.

e. Addressees are requested to give these instructions wide dissemination within their commands.

T. B. HILL [Rear Admiral, USN]
V. HAVARD, JR. [Captain, USN] Chief of Staff

Quoting from an official government report: (*The UFO Experience/A Scientific Enquiry* by J. Allen Hynek):

> The object was described as oval in shape with a slight rise on top as though with a canopy. Color was shiny...metallic and glassy. No lights were visible except that tops of trees appeared to glow white when the objects made descents... Object tilted toward the descent but appeared to rise horizontally and fly horizontally when it disappeared. Object was very clear to the naked eye with moon reflecting off it...estimated size approximately 25 to 30 feet across to approximately 10 to 15 feet at the thickest point. As object disappeared it took on an orange tint. No noise was heard....

This is what we hear from all those who have witnessed the maneuvers of the strange flying objects. There is no sound. The sometimes ear-splitting noise of Earth-man's mechanical devices is missing from this picture. There is only silence, mystery, and an awe-inspiring momentary look at a higher scientific culture, brought into our lives by those impossible unidentified flying objects.

Taken from *Unidentified Flying Objects*, we hear this from Dr. Puharich:

> ...We have a very good analogy in modern physics. For example, the so-called three-dimensional particle like an electron in a so-called tunnel effect. You see the electron here, and then it appears over there, instantly....This is one of the fundamental laws of quantum mechanics.[2]

Whenever Earth science talks about traveling in space, one of the supposedly huge barriers is the distance between worlds, measured in light years, our only measurement of the

---

[2] A mathematical theory in physics which starts with the assumption that energy is not infinitely divisible and deals with atomic structure and phenomena by the methods of quantum theory.

vacuum we call space (one light year equals 6,000,000,000,000 miles). Travel time to the closest planet is or was in Earth's mathematical compilation, measured in lifetimes. But now science is telling us that although we may not be able to reach the speed of light (186,300 miles per second), we may be capable of attaining 99.9 per cent or 185,299.99999999999999... miles per second.

Another thing that lightens the picture is *time dilation*, a part of Einstein's relativity theory. According to Einstein, time slows down as the speed of light is approached. But only for those on board a ship moving through space. At that rate we could, quite possibly, reach the center of the Milky Way (30,000 light years distant) in as little as fifteen years or as long as forty years, depending on the acceleration, while on Earth 60,000 years would have come and gone as we measure time. It seems that the result of the measurement depends on the state of motion of the system in which it is being measured, "...all processes unfold in different systems at different speeds." Here is some interesting information or space travel and time:

Time duration for crew in space	Time duration for inhabitants of Earth	Distance of point of return
1 year	1.0 year	0.018 parsecs[3]
2 years	2.1 years	0.075 parsecs
5 years	6.5 years	0.52 parsecs
10 years	24.0 years	3.0 parsecs
15 years	80.0 years	11.4 parsecs
20 years	270.0 years	42.0 parsecs
25 years	910.0 years	140.0 parsecs
30 years	3100.0 years	480.0 parsecs
35 years	10600.0 years	1600.0 parsecs
40 years	36000.0 years	5400.0 parsecs
45 years	121000.0 years	18400.0 parsecs
50 years	420000.0 years	64000.0 parsecs

---

[3] A parsec is 3.26 light years or 19,200,000,000,000 miles.

John Mac Vey (*Interstellar Travel, Past Present & Future*) suggests that there may be speeds exceeding that of light. "And if this is so then there must be another universe comprising particles unable to travel below the velocity of light, they must always travel with velocities in excess of that of light." We just can't detect them. But we understand these undetectable particles, the infinite energy field of the universes, the basis and builder of all energy has a name—Tachyon.[4] John MacVey goes on with an interesting supposition:

> What if an advanced galactic community has succeeded in harnessing the power and potential of the tachyon—an appropriately designed and constructed starship could then be accelerated to the speed of light, at which point the tachyon drive would take over.

I have no information on how Alan Landsburg came upon these particulars; it's possible that he was another of the Space Brothers' contacts. For all we know there may be many here on Earth. Regardless, this is the way Alan Landsburg (*In Search of Extraterrestrials*) describes a space ship:

> In the center of the disk shaped ship, with a domed cover above and below, is the navigational cabin.
>
> This may be compared to a large ball-bearing system, with about a quarter inch play in its movement. It can, never-the-less, remain absolutely stationary except for the continuous gyratory movement of the disk itself.

---

[4] Through the process of adhesion the atom, which is the building block of our physical universe, is a product of this energy. The formation of matter in our physical world is the product of a slowing down process caused by density.

Its reliability depends on the one hand upon the gravitational galactic waves (gravific waves) that vibrate in resonance with the lenses of the disk; and on the other hand upon a belt of radioactive material surrounding the central cell of the cabin that emits unstable nucleons.

The navigation cabin is spherical, transparent from within, but opaque from the outside, it is isothermal and resistant to both light rays and radiation; light can be seen from the interior but this interior itself is dark.

Inside is a central sphere some five feet in diameter which contains only the ship's instruments, the navigational aids, and proto-synthetic machinery. This central sphere is also the actual stabilizing mechanism; it prevents the ship from reacting to any gyratory movements of the disk which may be caused by cosmic forms of turbulence.

There are four radius vectors which are connected to the remote control apparatus that keeps the sphere in the exact center of the navigation cabin.

It should be noted also that everything in this cabin is weightless, so seats etc., would be of no use. It contains nothing but mooring ropes stowed all around its circumference to act as stabilizers while the ship is at rest. A hand-rail surrounds the machinery, so that all maneuvers can be carried out while the navigator supports himself with one hand.

Modification of gravic waves is affected by twenty-four lenses (twelve on either side of the disk) that switch on the apparatus. The various evolutions (starting, sudden stoppage and the enormous acceleration) are controlled by a titanium ring 'swimming' in a tube.

Gravific power, when used, acts simultaneously on every part of the ship and on every thing within its zone of influence If it is to be brought down from a height less than about 14,000 feet, an artificial electrical charge produced by the rotation of its disk is brought into action. The autonomous electricity is adjusted to the gravitational field of the planet that is to be visited.

For stabilization at a new space-time point, it has only to carry out the same maneuvers if the light distance to be covered demands it.

We hear this from Adi-Kent Jeffrey (*Parallel Universes*):

...it seems UFOs don't come from other planets or galaxies or go anywhere. They just appear and disappear as though arriving and vanishing through some interdimensional door.

'...The things we call Unidentified Flying Objects are neither objects nor flying,' Jacques Vallée claims. 'They can dematerialize, as some recent photographs show, and they violate the law of motion as we know it.'

George Adamski (*Inside a Flying Saucer*) agrees with Jacques Vallée. On November 20, 1952 there appeared in most newspapers, and many magazines, articles about a Californian, George Adamski, who, with a group of fellow beings interested in UFOs, was guided to a California desert where Adamski is said to have made his first of many contacts with extraterrestrials. What makes Adamski's account plausible—and palatable to the non-believers—is the fact that six friends, all professional people, witnessed the encounter and have notarized public statements to the witnessing. A testament. One of the witnesses made a sketch of "the man from Venus." Later Adamski authored several books that describe these meetings. Here he relates part of a conversation he had with his Space Brother, the man from Venus:

> Our ships perform feats in your skies which no Earthly planes of any nation can do. Your scientists know this. Your governments know this.... Many Earth scientists are hoping that in the not too distant future, they will succeed in building space ships like ours for interplanetary travel.

It seems to be happening. We hear this from Bruce E. DePalma ("Energy Unlimited," #5, August, 1978, *Science* magazine):

> The discovery of a new physical phenomenon, the N effect, which relates phenomena of magnetism, inertia, and rotation together in a new machine for the liberation of electrical energy directly from space is a pregnant development of a new age in science which will energize the civilization of the twenty-first century.

As of today our scientific capabilities have put men on the moon and sent searching machines out into space as far as Mars and Jupiter. And we believe that in this way we will be able, eventually, to communicate with, and perhaps visit, other dimensions, other inhabited cosmic worlds, just as ships and beings from other parts of the galaxy are visiting us. This looks to be our future. One thing we are very certain of—we are not alone. Where there are such advanced aircraft there must be highly intelligent life. This sounds like a feasible assumption to me.

Perhaps now, in an era of space frontiers, we can view the birthing of our world as a logical possibility totally divorced from being the product of a sorcerer's talents or the magical miracle of coincidence. We, with our ever expanding body of scientific technical knowledge, are capable of the first halting and timid steps toward building such a structure in space. Now we can begin to imagine older, more experienced beings implementing just such a design.

The world of intricately designed space stations has, for the last two decades, been moving across the drawing boards of our government engineers. This is the concept that Thomas Heppenheim, space travel engineer at the California Institute of Technology presented to the *National Inquirer*, September 1, 1975:

> The idea of a space station for 10,000 people is within the bounds of technology and is already possible. A group of twenty-eight professors and technicians who were commissioned by Stanford University and NASA to examine the problem came to that conclusion.

For that bright new world, Gerry O'Neill of Princeton University envisions a cylindrical vessel in space four miles in diameter and sixteen miles long. With air inside it spins on its axis once in 1.9 minutes, producing a centrifugal force exactly the equivalent to gravity on Earth. A person, he says, could stand up inside the cylinder and feel the same as if walking on level ground. However, the usual impression would be one of standing at the bottom of a rounded valley. Light will be brought into the colony through the use of mirrors (sunlight reflects off mirrors but cosmic rays do not). The valleys will be landscaped as meadows, forests, lakes, villages, and mountains, even to the extent of copying areas of Earth that are celebrated for their scenic beauty. The ends of the cylinders will be sealed to keep in the air. This will be done through the use of simulated mountains, some as high as two miles. They will be strange to climb. The lack of oxygen noticed on two-mile climbs on Earth will not be felt, and gravity will diminish rapidly as one climbs until a state of weightlessness is reached. Mountain climbing in space should be a fascinating experience.

Trees growing on the sides of the valleys would give the impression of leaning downhill, they would grow up toward the axis in the direction opposite to the centrifugal force. To brighten the habitat O'Neill divides the curved surface of the cylinder into six long strips each two miles wide. Making three of them transparent windows to bring the sunlight into the inhabited valleys.

Weather would result from the draft of warm air rising from the sunlit valley bottoms, and the sky will appear blue, giving a feeling of naturalness to the space habitat. And if this future colony is protected the way that the planners have designed, we are told it should be as safe as living on Earth.[5]

And while we are speaking of colonies in space here is one that favors the pedestrian. The Stanford Torus model is designed so that nothing will be more than two miles from any other part, "keeping the living area free from traffic." This from Heppenheim's *Colonies in Space*:

> The shield will be hollow...a shell of aluminum
> fitted around the Stanford Torus in the way that a
> bicycle tire fits around an inflated tube.

---

[5] The Moon can supply most of the mass needed in space for building. Sixty percent of the required silicon, aluminum, and oxygen could be obtained from the Moon. Fiberglass is an ideal material for use in space in the manufacture of lunar and space structural components and fiberglass can be produced from materials available directly from lunar soil.

According to Jerry Pournelle (*The Endless Frontier*) there are at least ten Earth-masses of building materials in the solar system: there are 200 tons of hydrogen, five tons of iron, 400 pounds of oxygen and 50,000 kilowatt hours of energy for each of sextillion people.

Carl Sagan and associates Khare of Cornell University and Eric Bandurshi and Bartholomew Nogy of the University of Arizona, claim to have discovered Cosmic Crude.

The shell will not be quite the same as a bicycle tire in relation to its inner tube, since it will not rotate. The Stanford Torus, the inner tube, will rotate once a minute. The shell will not rotate but will enclose the colony while the hull rotates past at over 200 miles per hour. The spokes would not appear as spokes, but as high-rise buildings twenty stories tall. Elevators move along the outside of the spokes in a glass enclosed tube. By relying on elevators and subway-like people-movers the colony's transportation needs can be met while eliminating those traffic nightmares we try to overcome here on Earth. It sounds good to me.[6]

In the past, in trying to cope with his own little galaxy, man managed to place his beautiful starship, Earth, right in the middle of a great and shining celestial world; it was all moving around him. Earth's glory was man's alone. Now all this has been changed, due to the scientific findings that relate Earth to millions of stars that can, quite possibly, claim the same ability to support life.

If there are civilizations other than our own in this universe (and we think there are) and if these other civilizations are older, more highly advanced (as it seems they should be) then, quite logically, they have been building space worlds more advanced than anything we can possibly dream up in or outside of science fiction. They must have space colonies. We might ask, are we one of them?

---

[6] "The entire manufacturing system consists of (1) a lunar mining and launching base to deliver raw materials into space; (2) a catcher in space to collect the materials launched from the lunar surface; (3) a space manufacturing facility that extracts useful materials from the lunar area and fabricates solar power satellites and other objects required to support and expand the system; (4) a staging base in LEO (Low Earth Orbit) that provides an interface between the Earth launch vehicles and the inter orbital vehicles; (5) habitats at each of these locations; and (6) logical support for the entire operation."—1977 NASA Ames Summer Study.

There are bright silvery fragments of light slanting through the fences we have built around our todays. A small wayward ray from our visionary tomorrows is penetrating our lives. The ancient history of Earth weaves its web around our plans for a future in space.

Man, who was, so he thought, destined to be earthbound, is now lost in the business of moving out into the strange universe which he was once firmly convinced did not exist. There seems to be a great joy in the abandonment to that age-old heavenly lure. There is a deep unfathomable need to join the stars, to find the source and follow the dream.

What is a Tree?

Said a child, "That man over there cannot see and he is asking, What is a tree?"

"Oh, I can help you," said a lumberjack. "Just hear my words and carry them back: trees make a forest and a forest is good, from them we get all the wood." "To make boats and houses," a carpenter said, "and things a fine lady lets go to her head."

"Trees make lumber," said the man with an ax, "all it takes is a few healthy whacks. Board feet when it's growing don't make a sound, but you'll hear the call 'timber' when it falls to the ground."

"Its limbs," said a small boy, "are sturdy and round. It makes it so easy to climb up and down."

"You tease," said the blind man, "You're fooling me. So again I ask, what is a tree?"

"Oh!" said the poet, whispering low, "you can tell by his face he still doesn't know. A tree's not a ladder nor is it a board. It's tall and graceful, you can take my word. It springs up fast and it reaches high, stretching its arms toward clouds in the sky."

"It helps us to breathe," said a passer-by, "without a tree we would surely die."

"A tree is green," they said. "And a tree is round—you can watch it grow straight up from the ground. It builds a house and it warms it too—I think we're telling you all we know."

The blind man was silent then he opened his hand, showed a small brown nut, said "I don't understand. Now tell me sirs how that can be, I have been told this is a tree."

6

AUTHOR'S CORNER—On Perspective

> Palongawhoya, traveling throughout the earth,
> sounded out his call as bidden. All the vibratory
> centers along the earth's axis from pole to pole
> resounded his call; the whole earth trembled: the
> universe quivered in tune. Thus he made the
> whole world an instrument of sound, and sound
> an instrument for carrying.
>
> 'This is your voice, Uncle,' Sotuknang said to
> Taiowa, 'Everything is tuned to your sound.'
>
> 'It is very good,' said Taiowa (*Book of the Hopi*,
> Frank Waters and Arnold White Bear
> Fredericks).

To all but a Hopi this is considered a legend, but to the Hopis this is a part of their ancient history, a thing that has actually happened, a fact.

If we can believe, which I do, that many things of a scientific nature were performed by advanced universal beings under the watchful eyes of a new and primitive race, we may find a basis for these stories.

Ignorance and superstition turned the works of the godlike visitors into miracles, and the miracles into legends and myths that have been created to explain the unknown, and passed down through the ages to become a part of our lives today. Now I should like to present some strange things that, depending on perspective, could be labeled legend, myth, or fact. More than a few of our contemporary myths are seriously considered to be science but still cannot be proven as a fact. And then we have those truths which are visually factual which some of us would like to think of as myth.

There is that 820-foot-trident placed on the cliffs in the Bay of Pisco. It faces heavenward and is constructed of white phosphorescent blocks that can be seen for miles out at sea. We might ask, what was its function, why was it needed?

One hundred miles inland on the plains of Nazca straight lines can be seen from the air laid out like a landing site. In between the lines are enormous animal figures cut into the desert, some as large as 275 yards long. But this overall picture can only be seen from the air. The question is, who was the artist and what was his purpose?

On Easter Island there remain hundreds of huge statues chiseled from lava rock, they stand as guardians around the Island and stare out to see as if waiting for the return of their creators. Who were the creators and why were they created?

Perched 12,500 feet up into the high plateau of the Andes Tiahuanaco poses yet another mystery. Magnificent buildings constructed solely of huge sections of stone, weighing tons, that had to moved from a distant quarry to the site. But how? Tiahuanaco is ancient, it was already a ruin when Pizzaro conquered the land. Who were the Supreme Beings capable of such a task?

Stonehenge is believed to date from 2500 B.C. and it appears that the formation has been changed many times through the ages. The mystery remains, what was the need that would make our ancient ancestors take on the task of transporting huge stones, sometimes weighing up to fifty tons, from Marlborough Downs, some twenty miles away, and why to this particular site?

The Great Pyramid in Egypt must be considered as a visual fact. It stands in the middle of our world for all to see, but the means and reason for construction are as mythical as any fairy-tale. To keep it within the frame of Earth-life reasoning, we have given out statements on its age, such as 5000 years. Along with this a notable authority tells us that this construction could have taken as long as one hundred years to construct. Then we are asked to believe that it was built in the lifetime of the Pharoah Khufu for a tomb at his death. All this is treated as "fact." Coming out of an Indian legend we hear this, "The Lords taught us that there is a place between life and void, that is subject to different time, and the Great Pyramid was considered a link with the second life" (*Gold of the Gods,* Erich Von Daniken).

The prophesies of the Great Pyramid acknowledge the beliefs of Ancient Ones bringing our past and our future together. We had only myths to advise us that Earth is a spiritual learning experience until those inquiring men of science stepped in, contradicting the old beliefs.

Peter Lemesurier brought forward the work of the earlier scientists who were of the belief that the Great Pyramid, far from having been fashioned with mathematical perfection to become a burial vault for an egotistical ruler, was, in fact, an accurate calendar of Earth events. In his work (*The Great Pyramid Decoded*) he has summarized events, dating the earliest at 2623 B.C., which he sees as the time the construction of the Great Pyramid was begun. The date AD 3989, is, he tells us, the "conclusion of the true millennium; the end of human escape into spiritual planes."

Edgar Cayce tells us that the construction of the Great Pyramid was begun in 10490 B.C.(sic). At the time of its completion it had sides of highly polished stone and a bright metal top which was the "hall of records." He claims that when this missing piece is uncovered—or discovered—it will contain a "sealed time-capsule containing ancient records and artifacts left by the Atlantean refugees and colonists who founded the Egyptian civilization."

Here we have another myth—Atlantis. Webster, in his extensive compilation of all facts interesting to the reading public, found it necessary to include this explanation of the mythical continent:

> Legendary island or continent supposed to have
> existed in the Atlantic west of Gibraltar and to
> have sunk into the ocean.

In the library of the Rosicrucians there lies a document which makes the statement:

> The Pyramid of Cheops, perpetuates the totality
> of Atlantean wisdom, whereas others reveal only
> part of it.

It is written that Atlantis, "the heart of the world," sank into the ocean with nearly all its inhabitants. According to Cayce's vision of Atlantis, it underwent three cataclysms. The first two around 15,000 B.C. divided the continent into islands; the second and last, 12,000 years ago, was the time of the sinking of the Atlantean continent.

Before the last upheaval there were those Atlanteans who emigrated to Peru, Egypt, Mexico, New Mexico, and Colorado. Those persons that escaped formed our present civilizations, and quite possibly the oldest of these civilizations is Egypt.

The sinking of Atlantis in the region of what is now the Sargasso Sea was, according to Cayce, caused by a combination of the natural forces of electricity and expanding gases that set off a volcanic eruption. The Atlanteans had discovered the secret of concentrating solar energy in a stone with "magnetic properties" that enabled it to emit more energy than it received. This, along with the destructive natural forces, was responsible for the sinking of the Garden of Eden, where man dwelt for ages in peace and happiness.

Cayce made the prediction that a record of the systems by which the Atlanteans manufactured energy would be found near Bimini, along with part of a temple. In 1970, the discovery of what is now termed the *Bimini Wall*, rising up from the bottom of the ocean, rescued Atlantis from the tight grasp of mythology, allowing it a place among our world's probabilities, a possible part of Earth's unknown and ancient history.

From childhood on we have had to deal with the mythical, accepting the fantasy images that we encountered in fairytales as part of our real world. Some fantasies have become facts, like that humped water-serpent, Nessie, that has taken over Loch Ness in Scotland. In the last half of the twentieth century our mythical world in space has moved from fiction to fact with the advent of something we might set up verbally as an "unidentified futuristic operation"—the UFO.

As visual phenomena UFOs would have to be classified as fact, even though most of what we have found out about these flying objects has been through stories and unconfirmed reports. Strange flying things in the sky are not new to Earth, however. This type of space travel is talked about in the early Hindu writings—the Vedas. These ancient sacred records not only tell of the gods moving through the sky in ships, they also give directions for building these space vehicles.[1]

For many centuries the stories coming out of those Vedic writings were considered myths and found interesting only by science fictionists—and, of course, eastern religions. Today, however, we attempt to send out messages to other worlds, we speak of space travel between worlds in terms of thousands of light years, and we seriously consider the existence of black holes, seeing them as possible doorways into other worlds—maybe even other dimensions of time.

We have come a long way since our belief system fed off the deductive talents of one of the great mathematical

---

[1] The International Academy of Sanskrit Investigation at Mysen, India, discovered an ancient treatise on Aeronautics written 3000 years ago including chapters, diagrams and materials, and three types of aircraft (*Gold of the Gods,* Erick Von Daniken).

minds of 1903. In October of that year a New York newspaper carried this observation made by Simon Newcomb, head of the U.S. Nautical Almanac Office, U.S. Naval Observatory:

> There are many problems which have fascinated man since civilization began, which we have made little or no advance in solving....May not our mechanicians...be ultimately forced to admit that aerial flight is one of that great class of problem with which man can never cope....

Many of the impossibles of yesterday are today a common part of our lives, such as air travel. Not only has Earthman touched foot on H.G. Wells' mythical Moon but there are similar plans for the planet Mars. A fully equipped lab has been floated in space, and just recently a shuttle system is being developed, a bus-like transportation to service the space station that the U.S. government will be building in space before the year 2000.

> It is not sufficient any longer to listen at the end of a wire to the rustlings of galaxies; it is not enough even to examine the great coil of DNA in which is coded the very alphabet of life. These are our extended perceptions. But beyond lies the great darkness of the ultimate Dreamer who dreamed the light and the galaxies (Loren Eiseley, *The Star Thrower*).

While decoding our human mysteries may seem of the most importance, there are those who keep reminding us that we are part of a vast universe and that our unknown past and our future are in space. "Our physical universe may be just one part of a large multiuniverse," says scientist and philosopher Morton Gale. Adi-Kent Jeffrey (*Parallel Universes*) explains the theory of many worlds moving in the same space separated only by the different vibratory speeds at which they move. Out of that comes this question, how is it possible to be unknowingly surrounded and affected by a universe completely inaccessible to any of the sensory perceptions? Gale explains it this way:

> ...the frog sits on a lily pad in the middle of his pond looking very much the master of his domain. The observer watching the frog may think the little jumper is seeing the same pond the onlooker sees. But not so. The frog's eyes respond only to sharp boundaries, convex curves that move, and changing contrasts in illumination, such as when a large shadow passes over him.
>
> In much the same way, other creatures of our world live in the same physical globe as we do, yet they are at the same time, not in our world at all, as far as their senses go.

Lobsang Rampa, a Tibetan Lama, tells it this way in *Twilight*:

> ...Everyone and every object on Earth has a counterpart of the opposite polarity in another galaxy, in another system of time altogether. This dual existence has effects, one upon the other, when a slit in one world comes into juxtaposition with a slit in the other. The slits become avenues of interrelation....

If we were to consider, seriously, this interdimensional activity between supposed parallel universes, we might be able to explain the mysteriously strange disappearance of individuals from city streets, mountain tops, wooded paths, open fields—right before our eyes, so to speak. They have been whisked off of boats, some have flown into oblivion and others have sailed—with whole crews—right through some invisible interdimensional door. There is no other way to look at it.

A great deal of information has come out in print about the "weird" goings-on in the so-called "Devils Triangle,"[2] and similar, though less frequent, happenings have been recorded as part of the history of the Great Lakes. Lake Superior has a notable reputation for that same type of unusual event. But quite possibly the hair-raiser of all time was a U.S. Navy experiment that was one of the best kept secrets of the Second World War.[3] Many writers have found that particular experiment interesting enough to retell it, but incredibly it was such a mind-boggler that it is generally repeated word for word by the different authors. This in itself should give it an aura of truth. A feeling of reality moves out of this strange experiment, and also in the equally unfathomable mystery that seems to surround and invade the lives of anyone who became involved in its story. This is the way Adi-Kent Jeffrey tells it:

> Briefly, the Experiment concerns the claim from a self-labeled eyewitness that in October of 1943 during World War ll, the U.S. Navy experimented with a destroyer in the Philadelphia Navy Yard. By applying the principles of Einstein's Unified Field theory, the U.S. Government attempted to teleport a warship from the Philadelphia Navy Yard to its home dock in Norfolk, Virginia.

> 'The effort,' asserted the witness, 'was successful. The ship not only dematerialized from the Philadelphia dock, then materialized at Norfolk in a matter of minutes, but it dematerialized out of the Virginia dock and then re-appeared back in Philadelphia...all, once again, in a few minutes.'

---

[2] *The Bermuda Triangle* by Charles Berlitz.
[3] *The Philadelphia Experiment* by Charles Berlitz and William Moore.

'...I saw, after a few minutes, a foggy green mist arise like a thin cloud.' This is the way the witness describes his experience. '...the D E 173 (Eldridge) became rapidly invisible to human eyes. And yet, the precise shape of the keel and under hull.. remained impressed into the ocean water.... (Sound) began as a humming sound, quickly built up...to a humming-whispering sound, and then increased to a strongly sizzling buzz—like a rushing torrent.'

The DE 173 (Eldridge) was launched July 25,1943, at Newark, New Jersey, and commissioned August 27,1943, at New York; according to the Navy Department's official records. Transferred to the Greek Navy in 1951, the records showed not only a discrepancy in the official launching (June 25th, not July 25th), but a displacement standard and full load discrepancy of some 660 tons. The only way that a ship can gain 660 tons of buoyancy is for something of that weight to have been removed. The witness had noted:

> ...there was enough radar equipment on the ship to fill a battleship including an extra mast which was rigged out like a Christmas tree with what appeared to be antennae-like structures.

The witness was aboard the Andrew Furuseth—a Liberty ship, hull number 491, built by Raiser Industries, Richmond, California—leased to the Noncom Navigation Company of San Francisco. Jeffrey tells us,

> "The achievement relating to the teleportation of matter was all that was hoped for... but it was the effect on the officers and crew of the ship that was the disastrous result of the Philadelphia Experiment, according to the witness."

Some went completely mad due to the shock of what Einstein called the unified force field. Others kept slipping back and forth between two worlds until they finally vanished completely. If we can ignore these terrible consequences of that trek into the unknown, we will find it intriguing to think that a few years ago, when we were actually just learning about radar, people voluntarily and through their own science had been able to pass through into another world, perhaps another dimension. Something did happen back there in 1943 that left distinct traces of a mysterious possibility of a still unknown quantity that finds its way into the minds of man. William L. Moore (*The Philadelphia Experiment*) tells us:

> ...Scientific units in private universities, some possibly funded by the government, are reported to be pursuing research in magnetic teleportation, with the attendant invisibility as part of the experiment. Some recent reports place such experiments as having taken place at Stanford University Research Facility at Menlo Park, Palo Alto, California, and at M.I.T. in Boston.

Today, man's oversized curiosity is leading him into the dark unknown. With a strange trembling in the heart, man is measuring his footsteps alongside those of his gods. Timeless space we are now beginning to conquer physically. We are now at the point of coming together, where the deep past catches up and leads the way into our space bound future. Space, one of yesterday's myths, is today's adventure.

This from Andrew Tomas (*On the Shores of Endless Worlds*):

> ...Eventually our space ships will reach the outer planets of the solar system, build bases on them and then venture further into interstellar space...

162

Are we moving from our all but vanished origins as a space colony to a global society capable of building space communities of our own? Will we, too, abandon our exhausted, exploited shell of a world to inhabit a new one of our own creation, a space station born of the need to preserve our specie against cataclysms engendered by our own errors? And, we might ask, did our extraterrestrial brothers and sisters go through this same period in their evolutionary climb?

Maybe, eventually, as Andrew Tomas sees it,

> On some unknown planet warmed and lighted by a white-yellow sun our astronauts may discover primitive life...the starships would come again and again....

It is not difficult to imagine another race of universal beings equally fascinated and determined to conquer similar obstacles.

Perhaps this has already happened in our solar system and Earth is one of those bases. Perhaps these unusual observations about our world would be more comprehensible if we were to approach these mysteries from the engineering standpoint of our own plans for a space station. Space is our final frontier, but no longer confined to the imagination of science fiction.

Ancient Sumerian stone tablets tell us that men from other worlds created our Earth. We are told that Man's history dates back millions of years, and in that time, man's world has been visited many times by miracle workers, scientific technicians, and visitors from heaven. From C. N. Ceram (*Gods, Graves and Scholars*) we hear this:

> The Sumerians mysteriously popped up out of nowhere highly developed, culturally and technologically.

Those same ancient records make the claim that Man is, through evolution and the science of genetics, the creation of those universal beings which early Man honored as gods. Recent advanced genetic sciences and technologies confirm the Sumerian concept of a gradual evolution and also that of biologically advanced humans as a result of genetic engineering and those same ancient writings make the statement that man is a descendent of those gods, and possesses godlike powers of which he is still unaware.

In our modern writings, world news sources give out reports on mysterious ships that move silently across our skies that seem to be keeping an eye on the humans who live on this blue planet. Are the gods returning? Do they, quite possibly, look upon us as universal cave dwellers, an immature race that has been cut off from a more advanced cosmic universal existence?

In my musings I can see that perhaps space colonizers moved across the limitless tracts of the universe, much as our pioneers of a century ago crossed the unknown American plains in covered wagons. And, like our pioneers, those space travelers stopped due to bad weather or mechanical failure, or because it was a place they liked—it fit their needs as individuals and as a community. This way small pockets of civilization emerged—collections of engineers, developers and settlers coming in or leaving for more remote regions. They were, at that time, interested in establishing way stations for their vehicles and in transporting personnel in the business of building new worlds.

The Earth's particular position was attractive both due to its distance from the sun as well as the length of the journey to or from a previously established way station, perhaps the

Moon.[4] Here was the perfect place to build in our galaxy. There were, as there are now, available "building materials" accessible directly from space itself, and those engineers were well versed in employing such unique energy sources with which we are only now becoming acquainted. They knew the secrets of gathering, transporting, and reassembling substances in the desired forms because they had erected numerous space communities before. The Moon was not built in its current location; it was moved into its present location to serve as a habitat for the engineers and their tools until the construction of Earth was completed.

But the position these galactic adventurers selected for this space community presented some specific computational difficulties. This was an unfamiliar area of the universe where a number of unusual energy fields intersected in a manner unknown to them. As a consequence, they had several failures in building this border colony and numerous tragedies and casualties in maintaining the outpost once completed. And, of course, it is probable they experienced the dismal finale suffered by so many civilizations which overextend themselves in their drive for expansion—their supply lines from home base thinned to nothing. This loss of contact, followed by a nuclear accident affecting some of their fusion reactors housed in the Earth's protective core, produced chaos. The survivors fled to the surface, bleeding and terrified, as the fail-safe mechanism sealed off the affected areas one by one.

Separated from their specialized tools and computers, and with no means to do much but survive, our progenitors

---

[4] Gravitation gives a shape to apparently featureless space. The Earth and the Moon, as one massive body, sit at the bottom of a completely gravitational valley. The Earth's well is 22 times deeper than that of the Moon. (NASA/*Space Settlements*, Library of Congress Catalog Card Number 76-600068).

had little left but the fragments of a language based on geometrical symbols. The triangles, circles, and odd crosses were scratched and painted on the dark walls of French caves, and later, in moderate form, became the glyphs depicting the Egyptian story of the underworld—all that remained of Eden before the gates to the garden were closed. Can we find Eden again?

Perhaps any possibility of reentering our actual points of origin on this planet—or space vehicle—have been forever closed to us. It may be that only through the risks we take (our future adventures into space) will we truly understand the seeds of our current world and the beginning of Man.

We hear this from James Kavanaugh, *The Birth of God:*

> Hammurabi is dead, so are Moses and the great prophets. Jesus too has died. The evangelists who applied his words to the problems of their day are dead. It is man alone who lives searching his own heart for the honest answers to the moral issues of life. He has outgrown the Ten Commandments that once bound a tribal people into a nation. He has outgrown the centuries of Christian legalism that forbade him to believe in himself. Now he has moved past the age of religious law into the era of personal responsibility.

166

Our World

Through my window, on the other side of a chain link fence, a man mows his lawn—the mower making a throaty hum. A child moves along the edge of this picture, stooping, picking up something, sometimes getting interested in that which he holds in his hand. Then, turning slowly, still finding something of interest in the object, he discards it—dropping it into a plastic trash container with an air of not being quite sure it should be treated in this manner. This action is repeated several times.

A shepherd dog races toward him, drops something in front of the boy then looks up happily, hopefully, but his playful spirit is ignored as the boy makes his way toward a slide, climbing up the smooth surface.

A woman comes out of the house, a bag on her arm. The boy calls to her as she steps into a car—she smiles back at him—the car moves down the driveway with just a small sound of an engine in motion—there is still the humming of the mower.

Our world. A spiraling planet in a universe of space. Man is a squatter on a space vehicle, his wagon hitched to a star-wars future.

Stephen Larson (*The Shaman's Doorway*) observes:

> ...riding the rim of the galactic wheel ten million miles a day we travel a superhighway that passes everything by but has no destination. The Earth, in fact and not fancy, is a space ship traveling alongside a star.

ADDITIONAL READING

Ardrey, Robert. *African Genesis* (Delta Publishing Co., N.Y., 1961)

Bentov, Itzhak. *Stalking the Wild Pendulum* (Bantam Books, N.Y., 1988)

Blavatsky, H.P. *Isis Unveiled/Science & Religion* (Theosophical University Press, Pasadena, CA, 1977)

Buettner, Janusch. *Origins of Man* (John Wiley & Sons, Inc., N.Y., 1968)

Clark, Arthur C. *Profiles of the Future* (Warner Books, Inc., N.Y., 1985)

Cronin, Vincent. *View from Planet Earth* (William Morrow & Co., N.Y., 1981)

Davies, Owen. *The Omni Book of Space* (Zebra Books/Kensington Publishing Corp., N.Y., 1983)

Eiseley, Loren. *The Invisible Pyramid* (Charles Scribner & Sons, N.Y., 1972)

Fahs, Sophia Lyon & Dorothy T. Spoerl. *Beginnings: Earth, Sky, Life,and Death* (Beacon Press, Boston, 1938)

Gould, Stephen Jay. *Ever Since Darwin* (W.W. Norton & Co., N.Y., 1977)

Greene, John C. *The Death of Man* (Mentor Books, 1961)

Halevi, Zev Ben Shimon. *Kabbalah* (Thames & Hudson, N.Y., 1977)

Highet, Gilbert. *Man's Unconquerable Mind* (Columbia University Press, N.Y., 1960)

Hodson, Geoffrey. *Hidden Wisdom in the Holy Bible* (Quest, Wheaton, IL, 1994)

Jeffrey, Adi-Kent Thomas. *Parallel Universe* (Warner Books, Inc., N.Y., 1971)

Johnson, Raynor C. *The Imprisoned Splendour* (Quest, Wheaton, IL, 1971)

Kavanaugh, James. *The Birth of God* (Simon & Schuster, Inc., N.Y., 1969)

Leach, Marjorie. *Guide to The Gods* (ABC-CLIO, Inc., Santa Barbara, CA, 1992)

Leakey, Richard E. and Roger Lewin. *People of the Lake* (Avon, N.Y., 1979)

Lord of The Shining Face: My House Is Empty

Leeming, David A. with Margaret Leeming. *Encyclopedia of Creation Myths* (ABC-CLIO, Inc., Santa Barbara, CA, 1964)

Lewin, Roger. *The Thread of Life* (A Smithsonian Publication, Washington D.C., 1982)

Montagu, Ashley. *Man: His First Million Years* (Signet Science Library, N.Y., 1958)

Nott, C.S. *Teachings of Gurdjieff* (Samuel Weiser Inc., N.Y., 1962)

Nouy, Lecomte du. *Human Destiny* (Longman, Green & Co., Inc., N.Y., 1947)

Ouspensky, P.D. *A New Model of the Universe* (Vintage Books, N.Y., 1971), *Tertium Organum* (1982); *The Fourth Way* (1971)

Pagels, Elaine. *The Gnostic Gospels* (Vintage Books/Random House, Inc., N.Y., 1989)

Pauwels, Louis & Jacques Bergier. *The Morning of the Magicians* (Stein & Day, N.Y., 1964)

Pearce, Joseph Chilton. *The Crack in the Cosmic Egg* (Simon and Schuster, N.Y., 1988)

Rampa, T. Lobsang. *Twilight* (Gorki Books, Div., Transworld Publishing, Ltd., Ealing, London, 1977)

Robinson, Lytle. *Edgar Cayce's Story of the Origin and Destiny of Man* (Berkley Books, N.Y., 1985)

Shiovskii, I.S. & Carl Sagan. *Intelligent Life in the Universe* (Delta Books, N.Y., 1966)

Sendy, Jean. *The Stairway to Heaven* (Avon Books, N.Y., 1983)

Sitchin, Zecharia. *The Stairway to Heaven* (Avon Books, N.Y., 1983)

Twitchell, Paul. *Eckankar* (IWP Publishing, Menlo Park, CA, 11th printing, 1982)

Umland, Eric & Craig. *Mystery of the Ancients* (Signet Books, N.Y., 1975)

Von Daniken, Erich. *Gold of the* Gods (Souvenir Press Ltd., London, 1973)

Walter, Kenneth. *A Study of Gurdjieff's Teaching* (Award Books, N.Y., 1969)

Waters, Frank, and Oswald White Bear Fredericks. *Book of the Hopi* (Ballantine Books, N.Y., 1969)